Practice Psychometric Tests

If you want to know how...

High Powered CVs
Powerful application strategies to get you that senior level job
This book will show you how to present yourself and your skills and experience in the best light, gain the recruiter's attention, choose the most effective format for your CV and project the right professional image.

Turn Your Degree into a Career
A step-by-step guide to achieving your dream career

'...offers a comprehensive range of advice; from finding out what you're good at, developing a career strategy and managing your motivation through to getting the job you really want.' – *Broadview*

Write a Great CV
Prepare a powerful CV that really works

'This book contains useful specimen CVs, covering letters and case studies, together with sample job ads, action plans and interview preparation tips.' – *Office Secretary*

howtobooks

Please send for a free copy of the latest catalogue:
How To Books
3 Newtec Place, Magdalen Road
Oxford OX4 1RE, United Kingdom
email: info@howtobooks.co.uk
http://www.howtobooks.co.uk

Practice Psychometric Tests

Andrea Shavick

howtobooks

Published by How To Books Ltd,
Spring Hill House, Spring Hill Road,
Begbroke, Oxford OX5 1RX.
Tel: (01865) 375794. Fax: (01865) 379162.
email: info@howtobooks.co.uk
http://www.howtobooks.co.uk

First edition 2005
Reprinted 2005 (twice)
Reprinted 2006

British Library Cataloguing in Publication Data
A catalogue record for this book is available from the British Library

ISBN 10: 1 84528 020 2
ISBN 13: 978 1 84528 020 8

Cover design by Baseline Arts Ltd, Oxford
Produced for How To Books by Deer Park Productions, Tavistock
Typeset by PDQ Typesetting, Newcastle-under-Lyme, Staffs.
Printed and bound by Bell & Bain Ltd, Glasgow

Contents

Part 3 – What Else Do Psychometric Tests Measure?

Acknowledgements

My thanks to the following people for their help and advice: Ben Maynard, Gerianne van Someren and Nicola Tatham of SHL Group plc, Daniel Shavick of Softwire Technology Ltd and Nikki Read at How To Books.

Introduction

The good news is there are thousands of brilliant firms out there, offering everything from sky-high salaries, profit-related bonuses, long holidays, flexible working, career-enhancing training schemes, staff discounts, free shares, free canteens, health and life insurance, gyms, outings, holidays … you name it. But first you'll have to get in.

Unfortunately the days when all you needed was a great CV and a sparkling performance at interview are long gone. Now you also need to be able to pass a whole range of psychometric and management tests with flying colours. That's what this book is all about.

In this book I explain all there is to know about psychometric tests; what they are, what they measure, why they're so popular with employers, if they're fair, what the pass marks are and whether or not it's possible to cheat!

Also included are **57 different practice tests incorporating over 400 questions** for you to try. If you want to improve your test scores dramatically, the best way to do it is to practise. Verbal, numerical, abstract, spatial, mechanical, fault diagnosis, accuracy, personality and online tests are all covered – just have a look at the contents section to see just how much is included.

I've also included a long list of useful books, and internet sites where you can find even more practice material.

By the way, the tests in this book are not 'made up' tests that you sometimes see in books about psychometrics, nor are they puzzles or quizzes of the magazine variety. They are genuine practice tests from the biggest test publisher in the world, SHL Group plc. This is the real thing. This is what you'll be facing when you apply for a job with virtually any medium to large size company, irrespective of industry, whether private or public sector.

As well as the tests themselves (and the answers) I also indicate the type of job for which each test is commonly used, information on what the assessors are looking for, and tips on how to improve your overall performance within each category of test.

My aim in writing this book is to give you both knowledge and experience, not just to survive, but to pass real live psychometric tests with flying colours. Job hunting can be stressful – but not any more!

Andrea Shavick, 2005
www.shavick.com

PART ONE
What are Psychometric Tests?

CHAPTER ONE

What Are Psychometric Tests?

What are psychometric tests?

Psychometric tests are structured, multiple-choice tests, taken in exam-like conditions, which aim to measure a person's ability or certain aspects of their personality. They are written by qualified occupational psychologists and used by thousands of companies worldwide to select staff. If you're looking for a job, chances are you'll be taking one or more psychometric test.

What do psychometric tests measure?

Some tests measure your ability to understand the written word, or to reason with numbers. Others measure your ability to solve mechanical problems, or follow instructions accurately, or be able to understand data which is presented in a variety of ways. And then there are the personality tests, assessing everything from motivation to working preferences.

What sort of jobs are psychometric tests used for?

Sales, IT, management, marketing, financial, retail, customer contact, clerical, supervisory, engineering, administrative, health, media, technical, practical and craft...in other words, all types of jobs, at every level, in every industry.

Which type of tests will I have to take?

In theory, all psychometric tests given to job applicants should be relevant to the job. You should only have to take, for example, a spatial reasoning test, if the job you are applying for requires good spatial skills. However, many organisations use verbal, numerical and abstract reasoning tests as a matter of routine no matter what the job description says. So be prepared to take more than one test, especially if you are applying for a senior position.

What's the pass mark?

All organisations using psychometric tests decide their own pass marks (which means there isn't a definitive answer to this question). Generally, you do *not* have to score 100% to pass. Many organisations set the 'pass' level as low as 50%. The whole point of the testing is to eliminate candidates who are totally hopeless, so they can concentrate on the rest of you...*unless* you are applying for a job for which the psychometric test is highly relevant, i.e. numerical reasoning for a finance job, fault diagnosis for an IT job. Then you really do need a high score to progress further along the recruitment path.

Are psychometric tests fair?

All psychometric tests, except personality tests, have clear right and wrong answers and are therefore free from the interpretation bias found in the marking of essay-type exam questions. Also, all applicants for the same job take the same tests. And testing is objective, unlike interviewers who have been known to favour candidates they like the look of. So yes, I would say they are fair.

However, if English is not your first language, or you're dyslexic, it may be a good idea to declare this before taking the test. The organisation might allow you extra time or grade your results more appropriately. Test materials can also be adapted for the visually or hearing impaired, but only if you alert the assessors of your circumstances in advance.

Why are psychometric tests so popular?

Psychometric tests have been embraced by many employers because it gives them an additional tool, over and above the traditional methods of interviewing, studying CVs and taking up references. Employers like psychometric tests because:

◆ they are a quick, easy and relatively cheap way of eliminating large numbers of unsuitable candidates early on in the recruitment process;

◆ it makes sense to find out whether an applicant is capable of doing a job *before* he or she is offered that job;

◆ candidates at all levels, from shop-floor to managing director, can be tested, short-listed or eliminated more or less instantly.

When will I come up against a psychometric test?

At any stage in the recruitment process, including first contact. These days many employers are so enthusiastic about psychometric tests, they put them on their application forms and websites (see **online tests** below). The tests are also likely to pop up later in the process when you go along for an interview, and if you've been invited to an assessment centre you'll probably face a whole day of them.

Note: 'assessment centre' is HR (Human Resources/Personnel) jargon for getting candidates together – either at the employer's premises, or an outside location, and subjecting them to an intensive battery of different tests and exercises. These could include role playing, in-tray exercises, group exercises and discussions, presentations and of course, psychometric tests. Sometimes the term 'development centre' is used instead. For more detailed information see my book *Psychometric Tests for Graduates*, also published by How To Books.

Where will I have to go to take a psychometric test?

For both ability-type tests and personality questionnaires you could be examined at your potential new employer's office, at an assessment centre, at an employment agency office, or in the comfort of your own home using your home computer (as in the online testing discussed below).

What are online tests?

An online test is simply a psychometric test you take sitting at a computer console via the internet, usually via your chosen employer's website. The questions come up on the screen and you click your answer choices using the mouse. Personality questionnaires, competency questionnaires, and ability-type tests can all be taken online, including those aimed at the very highest levels of management.

Online tests are most often used at the earliest stages of the recruitment process to sift applicants and pinpoint those individuals who may be suitable.

The advantage to you is that to take the test, you will only have to go as far as the nearest computer connected to the internet. Plus, you should find out if the organisation is interested in taking your application any further within a few minutes, which is a million times better than waiting for them to snail-mail you a letter.

The obvious advantage to the employer is that the candidate doesn't have to come into the office. Instead of spending money 'entertaining' large numbers of candidates, the employer can test candidates any time, anywhere, without having to lift a finger.

Can online tests be downloaded and then worked on at my own pace?

No. Most psychometric tests have time limits, and the ones you take online are no exception. You must work quickly because they are usually designed to time out after the allotted number of minutes. This is to prevent you looking up the answers at your leisure or consulting your best mate. Speaking of cheating...

Cheating – is it possible?

Tempting, isn't it? If your prospective employer can't physically see you, how do they know it's *you* taking the online test and not your best mate? When it comes to online testing, the answer is – they can't. However, if cheating does succeed in getting you further along the recruitment road, I'm afraid you'll be found out. Practically all companies who use online testing *retest* successful candidates further down the line, either at an assessment centre or at an interview. So if your online test score is dazzling but your interview test score is dismal, they'll know why. Be warned.

For lying, bluffing and second-guessing your way through personality questionnaires, see Chapter Eleven.

So how can I improve my psychometric test scores?

Practise, practise, practise. That's what this book is all about. It's amazing how far you can improve your test scores with a bit of practice, especially if you haven't taken many psychometric tests before. Practise also:

◆ Familiarises you with the psychometric test format so that you know exactly how to correctly record your answers on the day.

◆ Gives you confidence, because you'll know what sort of questions to expect (and what you're good at).

◆ Gets you used to working under time pressure.

◆ Trains your brain to concentrate – something most of us find very difficult to do for long periods of time.

◆ Speeds you up.

◆ Enables you to pinpoint your weaknesses, which you can then work on.

And that's what this book is all about.

CHAPTER TWO

Introduction to the Tests

How the practice tests are arranged

In this book the different types of psychometric test are arranged in separate chapters. Each chapter begins with the easiest tests and gets harder as you go along. I have indicated at what level, type of job, or industry, each test is used for.

At the end of each chapter there is a section dedicated to helping you improve your performance...and the answers of course, where applicable.

How to record your answers

Psychometric tests usually come in a multiple choice format. This means you will be given four or five possible answer choices for each question. Once you have decided which is the correct one, mark the corresponding box or circle on the answer sheet accordingly.

It is vitally important that you follow the directions precisely. If you are asked to fill in the box or circle, **fill it in completely**. Don't just make a little squiggle inside it, or tick it or put a cross through it. Most psychometric tests are marked by computers using a technique called optical marking. By indicating your answers in the correct way, the computer will be able to 'read' them. If you don't, the computer might not be able to 'read' them and you'll lose points – even if your answers are correct.

The same goes for the *number* of answers required. If you are asked to mark one circle, mark only one circle. If you mark two, the computer won't know which is your intended correct answer, and you'll lose a mark, even if one of the answers is correct.

Note: occasionally you will be asked for *two* answers – so read the questions very carefully.

How to speed up

Most ability-type tests are not designed to be finished in the time set. Giving you more questions than you can reasonably cope with in the allotted time is a deliberate ploy to put you under pressure. Taking a psychometric test is meant to be stressful. However there are a few tried and tested exam techniques which are helpful:

◆ Read the question very carefully. Sounds obvious, but it's all too easy to skim-read, make assumptions, and then get it wrong.

◆ After you've read the question, try to quickly work out (or estimate) the correct answer *before* looking at the answer choices.

◆ Narrow your choices by immediately eliminating answers you can see are incorrect.

◆ Only change your answer if you are absolutely sure you have answered incorrectly. First answers – intuitive answers – are usually the correct ones.

◆ Answer as many questions as you can. If you get stuck, take an educated guess. You cannot score if you leave answers blank.

◆ Keep working through the paper at a steady pace, keeping an eye on the clock. If you have time at the end, check your work and return to any questions you were unsure about.

◆ If you feel as though you are losing concentration, close your eyes and take a few deep breaths, then carry on.

How can I improve weak areas?

We all have areas in which we are not very adept. You may be a highly intelligent person but that doesn't mean you'll sail through the entire book without any problems. Some tests you will find incredibly easy, others will give you a very hard time. Most of the technical tests fox me, even with the answers right in front of my nose!

So whatever you do, don't despair if you find some of the questions difficult – or even whole sections – you certainly won't be the only one. Remember, **the whole point of this book is to familiarise yourself with the different types of test and give yourself the chance to practise, thereby helping you improve your performance.**

Note: Wherever you have difficulty with the questions, analysing them with the answers in front of you should make things clearer. And the hints at the end of each chapter should help too.

How to get the best out of this book

The most effective strategy is to treat the practice tests as if you were taking them in a real live interview situation. In other words, sit somewhere quiet, without distractions, and work as quickly and as accurately, and with as much concentration as you can. If you find it tough going don't worry, the more you try, the easier it will become.

Almost all the practice tests have suggested time limits. Set the clock, and attempt as many questions as you can in the time allowed, but don't worry if you can't complete all the questions. In the real world, *psychometric tests always have more questions than most people can handle.* It's a deliberate ploy to put you under pressure, to see how you work when under stress. Besides, working under a time constraint is good experience in itself.

Of course, there's nothing to stop you giving yourself more time, or attempting the questions as many times as you like – even after you've checked the answers.

You can also work through each test in its entirety, if for no other reason than to learn to concentrate. Remember that these tests are **practice** tests – when you apply for a job, the psychometric tests you'll take will generally be longer, with a lot more questions. Getting used to concentrating for longer periods of time will stand you in good stead and give you an advantage over the other candidates.

If you want to practise a particular type of test, the following list will help you locate the ones you want quickly:

Test List with Page Numbers

Remember – familiarisation and practice is the name of the game! Good luck.

PART 2
The Practice Tests

CHAPTER THREE

Verbal Reasoning

Verbal reasoning tests are multiple choice tests which measure your ability to reason with words. They are widely used in recruitment to select staff, simply because the ability to understand the written word is an essential skill for most jobs.

The simplest verbal reasoning tests assess your basic language skills: spelling, vocabulary and understanding of grammar. You are usually presented with four or five different words, or groups of words, and asked to pick the ones which:

✓ are spelt correctly
✓ are spelt incorrectly
✓ do not belong in the group
✓ mean the same
✓ mean the opposite
✓ best complete a sentence
✓ best fill the gaps in a sentence.

Here's a couple of examples:

Choose the words which **best** complete the following sentences:

All employees should . . . . from such a training scheme.
A result   B credit   C succeed   D enrol   E benefit

The insurance . . . . will . . . . if you do not pay on time.
A pollicy   B pollicy   C polisy   D polisy   E none of these
   laps   lapse   lapps   lapsed

What's being tested is your vocabulary, spelling and grammatical skills, and this type of test can range from basic school leaver to management level. The answers, of course, are both E.

Analogies are also popular. Author is to book, as artist is to:

A   paintbrush
B   gallery
C   painting
D   picture frame.

What's being tested here is your ability to recognise relationships between words. If an author *creates* a book, what might an artist create? The correct answer is C.

There are examples of this type of test at the beginning of this chapter. After that, the tests get somewhat harder. For higher-level jobs, your ability to make sense of, and logically evaluate the written word, is examined. These tests are often called **critical reasoning** tests, but in essence they are comprehension exercises. In each case you are required to read a short text, or passage and then answer questions about it.

However, unlike the comprehension exercises that you did in school, where the answers were obvious so long as you read the text carefully enough, critical reasoning tests generally require a little more brain power.

You are often asked to decide whether a statement is true or false, or impossible to verify, *given the information contained in the passage*. This last phrase is very important. Not only are you being forced to think very carefully about what you have read, you must endeavour not make any assumptions about it. You must answer the question using only the given information – something which is surprisingly difficult to do if you have any knowledge of (or an opinion) on the subject matter in question. Remember, it is only your ability to understand and make logical deductions from the passage that is being tested, not your knowledge of the subject matter.

The vocabulary and subject of the passage are often similar to those encountered in the actual job for which you are applying. For example, if you are applying for a technical job in IT, then any verbal reasoning test you encounter is quite likely to include the language, vocabulary and jargon prevalent in the IT industry. But whatever type of vocabulary is used, the level of understanding required is pretty high.

All verbal reasoning psychometric tests are strictly timed, and *every single question will have one, and only one correct answer.*

In this chapter

In this chapter there are 13 different verbal reasoning practice tests for you to try, of varying difficulty (easiest first, hardest last). Before each one I've indicated for what sort of job, or area of work you might be expected to take that particular type of test.

At the end of the chapter there is section entitled **Verbal Reasoning Tests – How To Improve Your Performance** which is intended to help you do just that across the whole range of verbal reasoning tests. Included in this section are some hints on tackling the questions themselves. If you have a problem with any of the questions then hopefully the advice contained in this section will get you back on track. Remember, however, that all of us have strengths and weaknesses, and everyone will have some difficulty with some of the tests in this book.

Test 1 Verbal Comprehension

This test measures your vocabulary and basic word skills using language which reflects the requirements of technical occupations.

This type of test is often used to select staff in technically or practically orientated jobs, for example, craft apprentices, technical apprentices, skilled operatives and technical supervisors.

Instructions: In each question, choose the correct answer from the five possible answers, indicating this each time by filling in completely the appropriate circle on the answer sheet.

Time guideline: There are 8 questions – see how many you can do in 3 minutes.

Choose the word which **best** completes the following sentences.

1 | All employees should [   ] from such a training scheme.

A	B	C	D	E
result	credit	succeed	enrol	benefit

2 | Hard is to soft as hot is to [   ]

A	B	C	D	E
cool	warm	cold	icy	tepid

3 | Which of the following words is closest in meaning to toxic?

A	B	C	D	E
putrid	poisonous	bitter	contagious	inedible

4 | All exposed pipes will have to be [   ] to protect them from freezing.

A	B	C	D	E
insulated	regulated	connected	incorporated	hot

---

5 | Which of the following words is closest in meaning to vertical?

A   B   C   D   E
horizontal   parallel   straight   perpendicular   flat

---

6 | Stay is to leave as advance is to [   ]

A   B   C   D   E
arrive   exit   retreat   come   hold

---

7 | A straight-edge should be used to ensure that the ends of the shelves are correctly [   ]

A   B   C   D   E
tightened   aligned   concentric   separated   flat

---

8 | Adept means the same as:

A   B   C   D   E
energetic   inefficient   enthusiastic   awkward   skilful

Test 1 Answer Sheet

	A	B	C	D	E
1	Ⓐ	Ⓑ	Ⓒ	Ⓓ	Ⓔ
2	Ⓐ	Ⓑ	Ⓒ	Ⓓ	Ⓔ
3	Ⓐ	Ⓑ	Ⓒ	Ⓓ	Ⓔ
4	Ⓐ	Ⓑ	Ⓒ	Ⓓ	Ⓔ
5	Ⓐ	Ⓑ	Ⓒ	Ⓓ	Ⓔ
6	Ⓐ	Ⓑ	Ⓒ	Ⓓ	Ⓔ
7	Ⓐ	Ⓑ	Ⓒ	Ⓓ	Ⓔ
8	Ⓐ	Ⓑ	Ⓒ	Ⓓ	Ⓔ

Test 2 Verbal Usage

The first of the verbal reasoning tests measures your vocabulary, spelling and grammatical skills, and also your understanding of written information. This type of test is often used to select clerical and administrative staff at all levels.

Instructions: In each question, choose the pair of words which best complete each sentence. Indicate your answer each time by filling in completely the appropriate circle on the answer sheet.

Time guideline: There are 8 questions – see how many you can do in 3 minutes.

---

1 Now the company had the [   ] to beat its main [   ]

A	B	C	D	E
opportunity	opportunity	opportounity	opportouinty	NONE OF
competittor	competitor	competittor	competitor	THESE

---

2 This [   ] has given us many [   ] for improving our products.

A	B	C	D	E
client	cliant	client	cliant	NONE OF
suggestions	suggestions	sugestions	sugestions	THESE

---

3 Results like these [   ] on careful [   ]

A	B	C	D	E
dipend	dipend	dipends	dipends	NONE OF
implementation	implimentation	implementation	implimentation	THESE

---

4 [   ] the attack that had been made on him, his speech was [   ]

A	B	C	D	E
Considering	Considering	considering	considering	NONE OF
moderate	modarate	moderate	modarate	THESE

5	The [　　　　　　] letter included many elaborate [　　　　　　]

A	B	C	D	E
original	original	originel	originel	NONE OF
sentences	sentence	sentences	sentance	THESE

6	I agree [　　　　　] your contention that the [　　　　　] should be favourably considered.

A	B	C	D	E
with	with	to	to	NONE OF
aplication	application	aplication	application	THESE

7	Costs are to be [　　　　　] by [　　　　　]

A	B	C	D	E
repayed	repayed	repade	repaid	NONE OF
instalments	instalements	instalments	instalments	THESE

8	The [　　　　　] is [　　　　　] if you do not pay the premium on time.

A	B	C	D	E
pollicy	pollicy	polisy	polisy	NONE OF
forfieted	forfeated	forfieted	forfeated	THESE

Test 2 Answer Sheet

	A	B	C	D	E
1	Ⓐ	Ⓑ	Ⓒ	Ⓓ	Ⓔ
2	Ⓐ	Ⓑ	Ⓒ	Ⓓ	Ⓔ
3	Ⓐ	Ⓑ	Ⓒ	Ⓓ	Ⓔ
4	Ⓐ	Ⓑ	Ⓒ	Ⓓ	Ⓔ
5	Ⓐ	Ⓑ	Ⓒ	Ⓓ	Ⓔ
6	Ⓐ	Ⓑ	Ⓒ	Ⓓ	Ⓔ
7	Ⓐ	Ⓑ	Ⓒ	Ⓓ	Ⓔ
8	Ⓐ	Ⓑ	Ⓒ	Ⓓ	Ⓔ

Test 3 Verbal Comprehension

This test measures your ability to interpret and understand written information. It requires a higher level of verbal skills than the previous tests.

This type of test is often used in the selection of individuals for clerical and administrative staff at all levels, for example, clerical staff, staff administrators, staff supervisors, secretaries and WP operators.

Instructions: In this test you are required to evaluate each statement in the light of the passage preceding it. Read through the passage and evaluate the statements according to the rules below.

Mark circle A if the statement is true given the information in the passage.

Mark circle B if the statement is false given the information in the passage.

Mark circle C if you cannot say whether the statement is true or false without further information.

Indicate your answer each time by filling in completely the appropriate circle on the answer sheet.

Time guideline: There is no official time guideline for this practice test, however try to work through the questions as quickly as you can.

> The cafeteria is open at 6.30am.
> Lunch is served between 11.30am and 2.30pm. If you require a meal after 2.30pm you must tell the chef before 2pm. Guests may be brought into the cafeteria if a special pass has been obtained from the Catering Manager.

1   The cafeteria is open at breakfast time.

2   You can have lunch at 1.30pm if you wish.

3   If you want a meal after 2.30pm, you must inform the Catering Manager.

4   The cafeteria is strictly for members of staff only.

All clerical staff should use form FPM2 to annually renew their security pass unless they wish to change any personal details. In this case, they should use either form FPM1 or FMP3. Form FPM1 should be used when staff members have been promoted, whereas form FPM3 should be used if other personal details have been changed, eg, address, department etc. Lost security passes must be replaced using form GMP2. The supervisor will supply this form when he/she is informed of the loss of the pass.

5   Mrs Jeffrey has lost her security pass. She should fill in form GPM2 to obtain a new one.

6   Form FPM3 should not be used to renew a security pass following a promotion.

7   Mr McCarthy has changed his address within the last twelve months. He should fill in form FPM2.

8   Staff must pay to have lost security passes replaced.

Test 3 Answer Sheet

	A	B	C
1	Ⓐ	Ⓑ	Ⓒ
2	Ⓐ	Ⓑ	Ⓒ
3	Ⓐ	Ⓑ	Ⓒ
4	Ⓐ	Ⓑ	Ⓒ
5	Ⓐ	Ⓑ	Ⓒ
6	Ⓐ	Ⓑ	Ⓒ
7	Ⓐ	Ⓑ	Ⓒ
8	Ⓐ	Ⓑ	Ⓒ

Test 4 Verbal Evaluation

This test measures your ability to understand and evaluate the logic of various kinds of argument.

This type of test is often used to assess reasoning skills at administrative, supervisory and junior management levels. It could be used to select applicants for a wide range of jobs, for example, office supervisor, senior personal assistant, sales and customer service staff, junior managers and management trainees.

Instructions: In this test you are required to evaluate each statement in the light of the passage and select your answer according to the rules below:

Mark circle A if the statement follows logically from *the information or opinions contained in the passage.*

Mark circle B if the statement is obviously false from *the information or opinions contained in the passage.*

Mark circle C if you cannot say whether the statement is true or false *without further information.*

Indicate your answer each time by filling in completely the appropriate circle on the answer sheet.

Time guideline: See how many questions you can complete in 5 minutes.

> Many organisations find it beneficial to employ students during the summer. Permanent staff often wish to take their own holidays over this period. Furthermore, it is not uncommon for companies to experience peak workloads in the summer and so require extra staff. Summer employment also attracts students who may return as well qualified recruits to an organisation when they have completed their education. Ensuring that the students learn as much as possible about the organisation encourages their interest in working on a permanent basis. Organisations pay students on a fixed rate without the usual entitlement to paid holidays or sick leave.

1   It is possible that permanent staff who are on holiday can have their work carried out by students.

2   Students in summer employment are given the same paid holiday benefit as permanent staff.

3   Students are subject to the organisation's standard disciplinary and grievance procedures.

4   Some companies have more work to do in summer when students are available for vacation work.

Most banks and building societies adopt a 'no smoking' policy in customer areas in their branches. Plaques and stickers are displayed in these areas to draw attention to this policy. The notices are worded in a 'customer friendly' manner, though a few customers may feel their personal freedom of choice is being infringed. If a customer does ignore a notice, staff are tolerant and avoid making a great issue of the situation. In fact, the majority of customers now expect a 'no smoking' policy in premises of this kind. After all, such a policy improves the pleasantness of the customer facilities and also lessens fire risk.

5 'No smoking' policies have mainly been introduced in response to customer demand.

6 All banks and building societies now have a 'no smoking' policy.

7 There is no conflict of interest between a 'no smoking' policy and personal freedom of choice for all.

8 A no-smoking policy is in line with most customers' expectations in banks and building societies.

Test 4 Answer Sheet

	A	B	C
1	Ⓐ	Ⓑ	Ⓒ
2	Ⓐ	Ⓑ	Ⓒ
3	Ⓐ	Ⓑ	Ⓒ
4	Ⓐ	Ⓑ	Ⓒ
5	Ⓐ	Ⓑ	Ⓒ
6	Ⓐ	Ⓑ	Ⓒ
7	Ⓐ	Ⓑ	Ⓒ
8	Ⓐ	Ⓑ	Ⓒ

Test 5 Technical Understanding

This test measures your ability to understand a written passage containing the type of material likely to be found in a typical technical setting, such as machine manuals and operating instructions.

This type of test is often used in the selection and development of individuals in technically or practically orientated jobs, such as craft apprenticeships, technical apprentices, skilled operative and technical supervisors.

Instructions: You are required to read the passage carefully, then, using the information provided, answer the questions which follow. Indicate your answer each time by filling in completely the appropriate circle on the answer sheet.

Time guideline: See how many questions you can complete in 2 minutes.

Company van use/allocation codes

Three codes exist for company vans:

001 – possess company van with full expenses paid
002 – possess company van with partial expenses paid
003 – has the facility to borrow a company van
004 – does not have the facility to borrow a company van

All senior members have 001 codes; 002 codes are automatically given to non-senior members after 2 years of relevant service and 003 codes exist for members who have not been with the company for two years but whose jobs include a high driving element. People with 004 codes tend to be those without a driving licence or individuals who rarely have the need for a van.

Test 5 © SHL Group Plc 2005 SHL and OPQ are registered trademarks of SHL Group plc which are registered in the United Kingdom and other countries.

1   Which code would a senior member with two years service have?

   A) 001.

   B) 002.

   C) 003.

   D) 004.

2   Members who only have one year of service but spend a large part of their time driving, would have which code?

   A) 001.

   B) 002.

   C) 003.

   D) 004.

3   Which facility is unique to code 002?

   A) The company van.

   B) Partial expenses.

   C) Full expenses.

   D) A borrowing facility.

4   An individual who has worked for the company for three years but who does not drive would be given what code?

   A) 001.

   B) 002.

   C) 003.

   D) 004.

Test 5 Answer Sheet

	A	B	C	D
1	Ⓐ	Ⓑ	Ⓒ	Ⓓ
2	Ⓐ	Ⓑ	Ⓒ	Ⓓ
3	Ⓐ	Ⓑ	Ⓒ	Ⓓ
4	Ⓐ	Ⓑ	Ⓒ	Ⓓ

Test 6 Verbal Reasoning

This test measures your ability to evaluate the logic of written information. It is designed for staff who need to understand and interpret written material with a technical context.

This type of test is designed for the selection, development and promotion of staff working in Information Technology and is suitable for applicants with A levels to graduate qualification or equivalent.

Instructions: In this test you are given two passages, each of which is followed by several statements. You are required to evaluate the statements in the light of the information or opinions contained in the passage and select your answer according to the rules below:

Mark circle A if the statement is patently true, or follows logically *given the information in the passage*.

Mark circle B if the statement is patently untrue, or if the opposite follows logically, *given the information in the passage*.

Mark circle C if you cannot say whether the statement is true or follows logically *without further information*.

Indicate your answer each time by filling in completely the appropriate circle on the answer sheet.

Time guideline: See how many questions you can complete in 5 minutes.

> Among the useful features available on this computer system is the **Notebk** feature. The **Notebk** feature organises lists of information in a record format. Its most obvious use is for lists of names, phone numbers and addresses but many other applications can be defined. One of the biggest advantages of using **Notebk** is that the files are stored in a format that can be used directly by other features. This means that files do not have to be converted or altered in any way.

1 The **Notebk** feature can only be used to organise lists of names, phone numbers and addresses.

2 If users wish to use **Notebk** files with other features, they do not need to alter the files.

3 The **Notebk** feature enables the user to instantly update lists of names and addresses.

Software engineering is an approach to the improvement of system productivity. In most circumstances, it has a modest impact on the productivity of the system during the initial development stage. However, systems developed using software engineering techniques have substantially lower maintenance costs and higher reliability.

4   Lower maintenance costs can be expected if the system used was developed using software engineering techniques.

5   Systems developed with these techniques are more likely to break down.

6   Software engineering is a widely used methodology when developing new systems.

Test 6 Answer Sheet

	A	B	C
1	Ⓐ	Ⓑ	Ⓒ
2	Ⓐ	Ⓑ	Ⓒ
3	Ⓐ	Ⓑ	Ⓒ
4	Ⓐ	Ⓑ	Ⓒ
5	Ⓐ	Ⓑ	Ⓒ
6	Ⓐ	Ⓑ	Ⓒ

Test 7 Verbal Evaluation

This test measures your ability to understand and evaluate the logic of fairly complex written arguments. This type of test is often used in the selection and development of individuals over a wide range of sales or customer service roles.

Instructions: The test consists of a series of passages, each of which is followed by several statements. You are required to evaluate each statement given the information or opinions contained in the passage, and select your answer according to the rules below:

Mark circle A if the statement is true given *the information or opinions contained in the passage.*

Mark circle B if the statement is obviously false given *the information or opinions contained in the passage.*

Mark circle C if you cannot say whether the statement is true or false *without further information.*

Indicate your answer each time by filling in completely the appropriate circle on the answer sheet.

Time guideline: See how many questions you can answer in 4 minutes.

The Osprey hotel chain yesterday confirmed plans to introduce a range of theme restaurants, amid speculation that it is facing severe financial difficulties. The concept was tested out in the flagship hotel during a three month period last summer. During that period the increase in average charge per head and the number of meals served surpassed all expectations. Competitors view the programme as the last feasible attempt to prevent this household name from becoming a distant memory.

---

1   The Osprey chain is about to close down.

2   Competing hotel chains believe that should this project fail, no other remedial action would save the company.

3   Estimates concerning the impact of the theme restaurants upon sales in the flagship hotel were accurate.

4   Osprey is a well known hotel chain.

Despite their aesthetic landscaping, ease of access and generous parking, out-of-town business parks have not turned out to be the attractive proposition that speculative developers had hoped. Their polished appearance and spaciousness have failed to compensate for limited provision of basic infrastructure such as shops, banks and leisure facilities as less scrupulous developers reneged on earlier promises or struggled with cash flow problems and other difficulties. It is thought that an expansion of home working, relying on advanced communication systems and technology, would make visits to smaller head offices situated in the heart of town centres more acceptable.

5 Proximity to retail outlets is seen as an important issue when evaluating office locations.

6 The continued popularity of business parks will be reinforced by new technology.

7 Cash flow is the main problem for speculative developers.

8 In certain circumstances, there have been discrepancies between the original plans and the finished business park.

Test 7 Answer Sheet

	A	B	C
1	Ⓐ	Ⓑ	Ⓒ
2	Ⓐ	Ⓑ	Ⓒ
3	Ⓐ	Ⓑ	Ⓒ
4	Ⓐ	Ⓑ	Ⓒ
5	Ⓐ	Ⓑ	Ⓒ
6	Ⓐ	Ⓑ	Ⓒ
7	Ⓐ	Ⓑ	Ⓒ
8	Ⓐ	Ⓑ	Ⓒ

Test 8 Verbal Test

This test measures your ability to evaluate the logic of written information. This type of test is used for the selection of graduates over a wide range of industries. It can also be used in the selection and development of work-experienced managers, professional staff, middle managers and senior managers.

Instructions: In this test you are given two passages, each of which is followed by several statements. You are required to evaluate the statements in the light of the information or opinions contained in the passage and select your answer according to the rules given below:

Mark circle A if the statement is patently true, or follows logically *given the information or opinions contained in the passage.*

Mark circle B if the statement is patently untrue, or if the opposite follows logically, *given the information or opinions contained in the passage.*

Mark circle C if you cannot say whether the statement is true or untrue or follows logically *without further information.*

Indicate your answer each time by filling in completely the appropriate circle on the answer sheet.

Time guideline: There is no official time guideline for this practice test, however try to work through the questions as quickly as you can.

> The big economic difference between nuclear and fossil-fuelled power stations is that nuclear reactors are more expensive to build and decommission, but cheaper to run. So disputes over the relative efficiency of the two systems revolve not just around the prices of coal and uranium today and tomorrow, but also around the way in which future income should be compared with current income.

1   The main difference between nuclear and fossil-fuelled power stations is an economic one.

2   The price of coal is not relevant to discussions about the relative efficiency of nuclear reactors.

3   If nuclear reactors were cheaper to build and decommission than fossil-fuelled power stations, they would definitely have the economic advantage.

At any given moment we are being bombarded by physical and psychological stimuli competing for our attention. Although our eyes are capable of handling more than 5 million bits of data per second, our brains are capable of interpreting only about 500 bits per second. With similar disparities between each of the other senses and the brain, it is easy to see that we must select the visual, auditory, or tactile stimuli that we wish to compute at any specific time.

4 Physical stimuli usually win in the competition for our attention.

5 The capacity of the human brain is sufficient to interpret nearly all the stimuli the senses can register under optimum conditions.

6 Eyes are able to cope with greater input of information than ears.

Test 8 Answer Sheet

	A	B	C
1	Ⓐ	Ⓑ	Ⓒ
2	Ⓐ	Ⓑ	Ⓒ
3	Ⓐ	Ⓑ	Ⓒ
4	Ⓐ	Ⓑ	Ⓒ
5	Ⓐ	Ⓑ	Ⓒ
6	Ⓐ	Ⓑ	Ⓒ

Test 9 Verbal Interpretation

This test is given to applicants for jobs in sales and customer contact areas. It's designed to test your ability to understand and evaluate the logic of straightforward written arguments. This type of test is suitable for candidates with A-level up to graduate qualifications.

Instructions: This test consists of two passages, each of which is followed by several statements. Your task is to evaluate each statement given the information or opinions contained in the passage, and to mark the appropriate circle in the answer section following the rules given below:

Mark circle A if the statement must be true based on the information in the passage.

Mark circle B if the statement is definitely false given the information in the passage.

Mark circle C if you cannot say whether the statement is true or false without further information.

Base your answers only on the information given in the passage.

Time guideline: see how many questions you can answer in 3 minutes.

> The international travel business has been hard hit in recent years, a problem that has impacted severely on the hotel industry. Despite this hotels are now fighting back by transferring attention from attracting tourists to attracting business travellers. One popular way of doing this is by creating an 'Executive Floor'. These floors are specially designed to provide business people with communal facilities such as personal computers, facsimile machines and photocopiers. Rooms on 'Executive Floors' are supplied with complimentary business magazines and newspapers, and more money is spent on decorating and furnishing these rooms than on other hotel rooms.

1   Rooms on 'Executive Floors' are decorated more economically than other parts of hotels.

2   More business travellers than ever before are now staying in hotels.

3   The hotel industry is how shifting its attention away from holiday makers.

4   Guests staying on the 'Non-Executive Floors' do not get free newspapers.

A new course aimed exclusively at training unemployed young people in sales and marketing skills has been started in the city centre by the CPU group. Financial backing for the course has come from the government and a local private enterprise fund. The CPU course can cater for up to 180 students at a time on either six-month or one-year courses. The CPU group already runs about 30 similar programmes, primarily in the south of the country. To be eligible, students must be unemployed, at least 19 years of age and have been out of full-time education for the previous two years. Depending on their personal circumstances, they may receive a cash allowance.

5   The CPU group has its head office in the south the country.

6   All trainees on the course are entitled to an allowance.

7   Funding for the new CPU course comes from a couple of sources.

8   Students completing any of the CPU courses have a greater chance of finding suitable employment than students from other equivalent colleges.

Test 9 Answer Sheet

	A	B	C
1	Ⓐ	Ⓑ	Ⓒ
2	Ⓐ	Ⓑ	Ⓒ
3	Ⓐ	Ⓑ	Ⓒ
4	Ⓐ	Ⓑ	Ⓒ
5	Ⓐ	Ⓑ	Ⓒ
6	Ⓐ	Ⓑ	Ⓒ
7	Ⓐ	Ⓑ	Ⓒ
8	Ⓐ	Ⓑ	Ⓒ

Test 10 Verbal Evaluation

The following test measures your ability to understand and evaluate the logic of written information and is used in the selection of staff working in a very large range of jobs, including supervisory, customer contact and administration. It is suitable for applicants with A-levels to graduate qualifications.

Instructions: In this test you are given two passages, each one followed by several statements. You are required to evaluate each statement in the light of the information or opinions contained in the relevant passage and select your answer according to the rules below:

Mark circle A if the statement is patently true, or follows logically *given the information in the passage*.

Mark circle B if the statement is patently untrue, or if the opposite follows logically, *given the information in the passage*.

Mark circle C if you cannot say whether the statement is true or follows logically *without further information*.

Indicate your answer each time by filling in completely the appropriate circle on the answer sheet.

Time guideline: See how many questions you can complete in 5 minutes.

Course for New Entrants

The induction course had a target of sixty hours, to be run for one hour per day for twelve weeks. The lesson time of one hour was considered to be the best length. It was thought that learning proficiency would fall sharply if lessons were longer and took place less frequently. At the end of the twelve weeks it was hoped that the trainees would have obtained the course objective of building confidence to cope with more complicated situations at work.

1   The course lasted 12 weeks.

2   A lesson time of two hours was considered to be the best length.

3   A target of 90 hours was set for the course.

4   These courses are beneficial to the entire population.

MEMORANDUM

To: All Staff
Date: 22 June
SUBJECT: New Filing Clerk

Despite the enormous strides forward in office automation, the amount of paperwork and consequently the amount of filing, grows and grows. Statistics show that, on average, a secretary spends twenty per cent of working time filing and during the course of one year creates at least five thousand new files. It is therefore this company's policy to employ a full-time filing clerk who will reorganise the filing system more efficiently and cut down the number of files needed by each department, thus freeing individual secretaries from this task.

For further enquiries about the above please telephone Ms Espey on Ext. 247.

5   This memo should be distributed to all staff.

6   Statistics show that, on average, a secretary spends a third of working time filing.

7   Ms Espey should be contacted for further enquiries.

8   All firms should employ a full-time filing clerk.

Test 10 Answer Sheet

	A	B	C
1	Ⓐ	Ⓑ	Ⓒ
2	Ⓐ	Ⓑ	Ⓒ
3	Ⓐ	Ⓑ	Ⓒ
4	Ⓐ	Ⓑ	Ⓒ
5	Ⓐ	Ⓑ	Ⓒ
6	Ⓐ	Ⓑ	Ⓒ
7	Ⓐ	Ⓑ	Ⓒ
8	Ⓐ	Ⓑ	Ⓒ

Test 11 Verbal Evaluation

The following test measures your ability to understand and evaluate the logic of written information and is used in the selection of staff working in a very large range of jobs, including supervisory, customer contact and administration. It is suitable for applicants with A-levels to graduate qualifications.

Instructions: In this test you are given two passages, each one followed by several statements. You are required to evaluate each statement in the light of the information or opinions contained in the relevant passage and select your answer according to the rules below:

Mark circle A if the statement is patently true, or follows logically *given the information in the passage.*

Mark circle B if the statement is patently untrue, or if the opposite follows logically, *given the information in the passage.*

Mark circle C if you cannot say whether the statement is true or follows logically *without further information.*

Indicate your answer each time by filling in completely the appropriate circle on the answer sheet.

Time guideline: See how many questions you can complete in 5 minutes.

USE OF THE TELEPHONE

The telephone is the executive's most used tool. A survey has shown that, in Britain, executives make around thirty-nine business calls a day in the south, and approximately thirty-one per day in the north. However, fifty-three per cent of the executives surveyed also complained of wasting a lot of time on the phone through waiting for calls, returning calls, or simply not getting through. International telephones are working on a computerised system which should help to eliminate some of these problems, but one should not expect this change within the next decade.

1 According to the survey, executives in the north make around 39 business calls a day.

2 The telephone will always be the executive's most used tool.

3 Over half of the executives in the survey said that they waste a lot of time on the telephone.

4 Telephones are often misused.

SAFARI PARK SAFETY

When visiting a safari park visitors are reminded of the importance of keeping their car windows closed. Many accidents have occurred through visitors winding down their car windows to take photographs. Baboons have then gained access to the car interior with disastrous results. In some cases, the visitors actually step out of the car and take a closer look at the wild animals, resulting in serious injury. Signs warning of these and other dangers are sited every five hundred yards around the park. Safari park advisors are at a loss to know what other measures to take to warn the public of the dangers of wild animals.

5   Visitors sometimes get out of their car to look more closely at the animals.

6   Accidents have occurred when visitors wind down their windows to take photographs.

7   'Danger' signs are placed every 50 yards around the park.

8   The general public should be banned from safari parks.

Test 11 Answer Sheet

	A	B	C
1	Ⓐ	Ⓑ	Ⓒ
2	Ⓐ	Ⓑ	Ⓒ
3	Ⓐ	Ⓑ	Ⓒ
4	Ⓐ	Ⓑ	Ⓒ
5	Ⓐ	Ⓑ	Ⓒ
6	Ⓐ	Ⓑ	Ⓒ
7	Ⓐ	Ⓑ	Ⓒ
8	Ⓐ	Ⓑ	Ⓒ

Test 12 Verbal Evaluation

The following test measures your ability to understand and evaluate the logic of written information and is used in the selection of staff working in a very large range of jobs, including supervisory, customer contact and administration. It is suitable for applicants with A-levels to graduate qualifications.

Instructions: In this test you are given two passages, each one followed by several statements. You are required to evaluate each statement in the light of the information or opinions contained in the relevant passage and select your answer according to the rules below:

Mark circle A if the statement is patently true, or follows logically *given the information in the passage.*

Mark circle B if the statement is patently untrue, or if the opposite follows logically, *given the information in the passage.*

Mark circle C if you cannot say whether the statement is true or follows logically *without further information.*

Indicate your answer each time by filling in completely the appropriate circle on the answer sheet.

Time guideline: See how many questions you can complete in 5 minutes.

> ### PASSIVE SMOKING
>
> A few years ago complaints about pollution in the office by tobacco smoke would not have been taken seriously. However, recent evidence published in medical journals suggests that even 'secondary inhalation' (breathing in someone else's smoke) can put non-smokers at an increased risk from the harmful properties of tobacco smoke. This makes them more susceptible to chest and respiratory problems than non-smokers living and working in smoke-free environments.

1 In the past, complaints about tobacco smoke pollution would have been treated seriously.

2 'Secondary inhalation' is breathing in another's smoke.

3 Medical journals have proposed that smoking should be banned from offices.

4 Smokers have an increased risk of heart disease.

Test 12 SHL © Group Plc 2005 SHL and OPQ are registered trademarks of SHL Group plc which are registered in the United Kingdom and other countries.

> ## How to Encourage a Child's Interest in Education
>
> To help stimulate their child's interest in education, wise parents should become involved starting from the child's first day of school. The child's drawings should be praised and subsequent help given with homework. This should create an enjoyable habit of seeking knowledge for knowledge's sake, rather than a chore to be finished before the child may watch television or go out to play. Close communication between teachers and parents is also beneficial to the child as possible problems on both sides can be discussed and resolved to the child's advantage.

5 Wise parents should praise their child's drawings.

6 Teachers and parents should avoid talking to each other.

7 All children watch television.

8 All children should go to play school.

Test 12 Answer Sheet

	A	B	C
1	Ⓐ	Ⓑ	Ⓒ
2	Ⓐ	Ⓑ	Ⓒ
3	Ⓐ	Ⓑ	Ⓒ
4	Ⓐ	Ⓑ	Ⓒ
5	Ⓐ	Ⓑ	Ⓒ
6	Ⓐ	Ⓑ	Ⓒ
7	Ⓐ	Ⓑ	Ⓒ
8	Ⓐ	Ⓑ	Ⓒ

Test 13 Verbal Evaluation

The following test measures your ability to understand and evaluate the logic of written information and is used in the selection of staff working in a very large range of jobs, including supervisory, customer contact and administration. It is suitable for applicants with A-levels to graduate qualifications.

Instructions: In this test you are given one passage, followed by several statements. You are required to evaluate each statement in the light of the information or opinions contained in the passage and select your answer according to the rules below:

Mark circle A if the statement is patently **true**, or follows logically *given the information in the passage.*

Mark circle B if the statement is patently **untrue**, or if the opposite follows logically, *given the information in the passage.*

Mark circle C if you **cannot say** whether the statement is true or follows logically *without further information.*

Indicate your answer each time by filling in completely the appropriate circle on the answer sheet.

Time guideline: See how many questions you can complete in 5 minutes.

Women as Seen on Television

Despite the fact that sixty per cent of Britain's married women have their own careers, fiction and television writers still refer to wives in such terms as 'her indoors' or portray them as downtrodden slaves at the kitchen sink, surrounded by hordes of grubby kids. By comparison, television adverts show sparkling clean kitchens with housewives surrounded by 2.3 freshly scrubbed children in a germ-free environment. Neither of these two descriptions portrays the reality of working married women in today's society: it is thought that until women themselves hold the top posts in the television industry, these views will remain unchanged.

1 Sixty per cent of Britain's married women have their own careers.

2 Television writers never refer to wives as 'her indoors'.

3 Women hold all the top posts in the television industry.

4 The National Statistics show that most couples have 2.3 children.

Test 13 Answer Sheet

	A	B	C
1	Ⓐ	Ⓑ	Ⓒ
2	Ⓐ	Ⓑ	Ⓒ
3	Ⓐ	Ⓑ	Ⓒ
4	Ⓐ	Ⓑ	Ⓒ

Answers to Verbal Reasoning questions

Test 1 Verbal Comprehension

	A	B	C	D	E
1	Ⓐ	Ⓑ	Ⓒ	Ⓓ	●
2	Ⓐ	Ⓑ	●	Ⓓ	Ⓔ
3	Ⓐ	●	Ⓒ	Ⓓ	Ⓔ
4	●	Ⓑ	Ⓒ	Ⓓ	Ⓔ
5	Ⓐ	Ⓑ	Ⓒ	●	Ⓔ
6	Ⓐ	Ⓑ	●	Ⓓ	Ⓔ
7	Ⓐ	●	Ⓒ	Ⓓ	Ⓔ
8	Ⓐ	Ⓑ	Ⓒ	Ⓓ	●

Test 2 Verbal Usage

	A	B	C	D	E
1	Ⓐ	●	Ⓒ	Ⓓ	Ⓔ
2	●	Ⓑ	Ⓒ	Ⓓ	Ⓔ
3	Ⓐ	Ⓑ	Ⓒ	Ⓓ	●
4	●	Ⓑ	Ⓒ	Ⓓ	Ⓔ
5	●	Ⓑ	Ⓒ	Ⓓ	Ⓔ
6	Ⓐ	●	Ⓒ	Ⓓ	Ⓔ
7	Ⓐ	Ⓑ	Ⓒ	●	Ⓔ
8	Ⓐ	Ⓑ	Ⓒ	Ⓓ	●

Test 3 Verbal Comprehension

	A	B	C
1	●	Ⓑ	Ⓒ
2	●	Ⓑ	Ⓒ
3	Ⓐ	●	Ⓒ
4	Ⓐ	●	Ⓒ
5	●	Ⓑ	Ⓒ
6	●	Ⓑ	Ⓒ
7	Ⓐ	●	Ⓒ
8	Ⓐ	Ⓑ	●

Test 4 Verbal Evaluation

	A	B	C
1	●	Ⓑ	Ⓒ
2	Ⓐ	●	Ⓒ
3	Ⓐ	Ⓑ	●
4	●	Ⓑ	Ⓒ
5	Ⓐ	Ⓑ	●
6	Ⓐ	●	Ⓒ
7	Ⓐ	●	Ⓒ
8	●	Ⓑ	Ⓒ

Test 5 Technical Understanding

	A	B	C	D
1	●	Ⓑ	Ⓒ	Ⓓ
2	Ⓐ	Ⓑ	●	Ⓓ
3	Ⓐ	●	Ⓒ	Ⓓ
4	Ⓐ	Ⓑ	Ⓒ	●

Test 6 Verbal Reasoning

	A	B	C
1	Ⓐ	●	Ⓒ
2	●	Ⓑ	Ⓒ
3	Ⓐ	Ⓑ	●
4	●	Ⓑ	Ⓒ
5	Ⓐ	●	Ⓒ
6	Ⓐ	Ⓑ	●

Test 7 Verbal Evaluation

	A	B	C
1	Ⓐ	Ⓑ	●
2	●	Ⓑ	Ⓒ
3	Ⓐ	●	Ⓒ
4	●	Ⓑ	Ⓒ
5	●	Ⓑ	Ⓒ
6	Ⓐ	●	Ⓒ
7	Ⓐ	Ⓑ	●
8	●	Ⓑ	Ⓒ

Test 8 Verbal Test

	A	B	C
1	Ⓐ	Ⓑ	●
2	Ⓐ	●	Ⓒ
3	●	Ⓑ	Ⓒ
4	Ⓐ	Ⓑ	●
5	Ⓐ	●	Ⓒ
6	Ⓐ	Ⓑ	●

Test 9 Verbal Interpretation

	A	B	C
1	Ⓐ	●	Ⓒ
2	Ⓐ	Ⓑ	●
3	●	Ⓑ	Ⓒ
4	Ⓐ	Ⓑ	●
5	Ⓐ	Ⓑ	●
6	Ⓐ	●	Ⓒ
7	●	Ⓑ	Ⓒ
8	Ⓐ	Ⓑ	●

Test 10 Verbal Evaluation

	A	B	C
1	●	Ⓑ	Ⓒ
2	Ⓐ	●	Ⓒ
3	Ⓐ	●	Ⓒ
4	Ⓐ	Ⓑ	●
5	●	Ⓑ	Ⓒ
6	Ⓐ	●	Ⓒ
7	●	Ⓑ	Ⓒ
8	Ⓐ	Ⓑ	●

Test 11 Verbal Evaluation

	A	B	C
1	Ⓐ	●	Ⓒ
2	Ⓐ	Ⓑ	●
3	●	Ⓑ	Ⓒ
4	Ⓐ	Ⓑ	●
5	●	Ⓑ	Ⓒ
6	●	Ⓑ	Ⓒ
7	Ⓐ	●	Ⓒ
8	Ⓐ	Ⓑ	●

Test 12 Verbal Evaluation

	A	B	C
1	Ⓐ	●	Ⓒ
2	●	Ⓑ	Ⓒ
3	Ⓐ	Ⓑ	●
4	Ⓐ	Ⓑ	●
5	●	Ⓑ	Ⓒ
6	Ⓐ	●	Ⓒ
7	Ⓐ	Ⓑ	●
8	Ⓐ	Ⓑ	●

Test 13 Verbal Evaluation

	A	B	C
1	●	Ⓑ	Ⓒ
2	Ⓐ	●	Ⓒ
3	Ⓐ	●	Ⓒ
4	Ⓐ	Ⓑ	●

Verbal reasoning tests – how to improve your performance

◆ Read books and newspapers.

◆ Whenever you are uncertain how to spell a particular word, look it up. The more you do this, the more your spelling will improve.

◆ Do verbal problem-solving exercises such as crosswords.

◆ If applying for a managerial position, read reports and business journals, especially those concerning the industry to which you are applying.

◆ If applying for a technical job, read technical manuals and instruction books.

◆ When attempting verbal tests that measure your ability to spell, your intuitive first guess is likely to be the correct one. If you spend too long staring at the words, they'll all look wrong – even the ones which are spelt correctly.

◆ In critical reasoning tests, always read the passage thoroughly. Don't skip through sections, or scan the text at high speed. Reading with understanding requires concentrated effort – not an easy thing to do however good your reading skills. Re-read anything of which you are unsure.

◆ Also read the questions themselves very carefully to ensure you understand exactly what it is you are being asked.

◆ Look at the answer choices and quickly eliminate any you know to be incorrect. Concentrate your energies on deciding between the most likely possibilities.

◆ Think carefully before selecting an answer which includes words like *always*, *never*, *true*, *false*, *none* and *all*. These words leave no room for manoeuvre or any exception whatsoever.

◆ Answer the questions using only the given information. Don't let prior knowledge or your opinion on the subject matter influence you. Only your ability to understand and make logical deductions *from the passage* is being tested.

◆ Verbal reasoning tests demand a high level of concentration, so treat yourself to a break every now and then. Sit up straight, shut your eyes and take a few deep breaths, just for 20 seconds or so. This will calm you down, relax your back and give your eyes and brain a well deserved rest.

- If you really feel a question is misleading, ambiguous, or simply wrong, make an educated guess and move on. Mistakes do crop up occasionally, well occupational psychologists are only human after all!

CHAPTER 4

Numerical Reasoning

Numerical reasoning tests are multiple-choice psychometric tests which are used as part of the selection procedure for jobs with any element of figure work. This includes a wide range of jobs, such as those dealing with money, buying, administration, engineering, statistics, analytical science, and any sort of numerical calculations.

In addition, psychometric tests which measure *basic* mathematical ability are also becoming more and more commonplace simply because employers want to know whether you are numerate or not. So even if you would never dream of applying for a job with any sort of figure work, I would still recommend you work through this chapter if only to improve your concentrating skills and exam technique.

Numerical reasoning questions can be presented in a variety of different ways, including:

- basic maths
- sequences (usually numbers but can also be letters of the alphabet)
- number problems
- numerical estimation problems
- data interpretation using tables, graphs and diagrams

and varying levels of difficulty. Some allow you the use of a calculator, others do not. All numerical reasoning tests are strictly timed, and *most* questions will have *one, and only one correct answer* (occasionally you find a question that requires *two* answers).

In this chapter

In this chapter there are 17 different numerical psychometric tests for you to try (easiest first, hardest last). Before each one I've indicated for what sort of job, or industry you might be expected to take that particular type of test.

At the end of the chapter there is section entitled **Numerical Tests – How To Improve Your Performance** which is intended to help you do just that across the whole range of numerical tests. Included in this section are some hints on tackling the questions themselves. If you have a problem with any of the questions then hopefully the advice contained in this section will get you back on track. Remember, however, that all of us have strengths and weaknesses, and everyone will have some difficulty with some of the tests in this book.

Note: do not use a calculator unless specifically instructed to.

Test 14 Number Skills

This test measures very basic number skills. It is used in the selection of individuals in technically or practically oriented jobs such as apprentices and skilled operatives, and for any job where quick and accurate calculations are required.

Instructions: For each question you are to calculate the answer and decide which of the four answers given is correct and fill in completely the appropriate circle A, B, C or D on the answer sheet.

Time guideline: There is no official time limit for this test, however try to complete the questions in 1 minute.

A	B	C	D

	A	B	C	D
1. 75 + 10 =	90	85	60	100

	A	B	C	D
2. 27 ÷ 3 =	21	6	9	30

	A	B	C	D
3. 19 − 7 =	26	23	16	12

Test 14 Answer Sheet

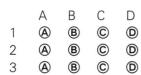

	A	B	C	D
1	Ⓐ	Ⓑ	Ⓒ	Ⓓ
2	Ⓐ	Ⓑ	Ⓒ	Ⓓ
3	Ⓐ	Ⓑ	Ⓒ	Ⓓ

Test 15 Numerical Computation

The first of the numerical reasoning tests is called a **numerical computation** test, a rather fancy name for basic maths. The emphasis is on understanding numerical relationships and operations, as well as on quick and accurate calculation.

This type of test is often used in the selection and development of individuals in technically or practically orientated jobs such as craft apprentices, technical apprentices, skilled operatives and technical supervisors.

Instructions: In each question find the number which should replace the question mark. Indicate your answer by filling in completely the appropriate circle on the answer sheet. *Do not use a calculator.*

Time guideline: There are 10 questions – see how many you can do in 3 minutes. Remember to work accurately as well as quickly.

		A	B	C	D	E
1	46 − ? = 17	17	19	27	29	39

		A	B	C	D	E
2	180 ÷ 30 = ?	6	8	10	12	15

		A	B	C	D	E
3	6 × ? = 45	5.5	6.5	7.5	8	9

		A	B	C	D	E
4	15 + 49 = 4 + ?	15	24	32	50	60

		A	B	C	D	E
5	$^3/_5$ × ? = $^1/_5$	$^1/_6$	$^1/_4$	$^1/_3$	$^1/_2$	$^2/_3$

		A	B	C	D	E
6	35.6 + 2.43 = ?	37.3	38.03	38.9	39.13	39.63

		A	B	C	D	E
7	60% of 20 = ?	12	13	14	15	16

		A	B	C	D	E
8	0.1 × 0.1 = . ?	0.0011	0.01	0.1	0.11	1.0

		A	B	C	D	E
9	0.8 ÷ 0.2 = ?	0.16	0.25	0.4	4.0	16.0

		A	B	C	D	E
10	17 × 16 = ? × 8	18	19	25	34	40

Test 15 Answer Sheet

	A	B	C	D	E
1	Ⓐ	Ⓑ	Ⓒ	Ⓓ	Ⓔ
2	Ⓐ	Ⓑ	Ⓒ	Ⓓ	Ⓔ
3	Ⓐ	Ⓑ	Ⓒ	Ⓓ	Ⓔ
4	Ⓐ	Ⓑ	Ⓒ	Ⓓ	Ⓔ
5	Ⓐ	Ⓑ	Ⓒ	Ⓓ	Ⓔ
6	Ⓐ	Ⓑ	Ⓒ	Ⓓ	Ⓔ
7	Ⓐ	Ⓑ	Ⓒ	Ⓓ	Ⓔ
8	Ⓐ	Ⓑ	Ⓒ	Ⓓ	Ⓔ
9	Ⓐ	Ⓑ	Ⓒ	Ⓓ	Ⓔ
10	Ⓐ	Ⓑ	Ⓒ	Ⓓ	Ⓔ

Test 16 Numerical Computation

Now try another numerical computation test. This measures basic number skills with the emphasis on straightforward calculation.

This type of test is often used in the selection of individuals for clerical and administrative staff at all levels, for example, clerical staff, staff administrators, staff supervisors, secretaries and WP operators.

Instructions: As in the previous test, find the number which should replace the question mark. Indicate your answer by filling in completely the appropriate circle on the answer sheet. *Do not use a calculator.*

Time guideline: There are 9 questions – see how many you can do in 3 minutes. Remember to work accurately as well as quickly.

1	23	+	58	=	?

	A	B	C	D	E
	71	81	85	91	95

2	28	÷	4	=	?

	A	B	C	D	E
	5	6	7	8	9

3	?	=	1.5	×	2.5

	A	B	C	D	E
	2.5	2.75	3.00	3.5	3.75

4	68	–	29	=	114	–	?

	A	B	C	D	E
	39	65	68	75	85

	A	B	C	D	E
	$1/15$	$1/8$	$2/15$	$1/2$	$3/5$

5	$1/3$	−	$1/5$	=	?

	A	B	C	D	E
	9	10	11	12	13

6	17	×	?	=	204

	A	B	C	D	E
	9	9.5	10	10.5	11

7	132	÷	?	=	12

	A	B	C	D	E
	28	31	38	41	48

8	16	+	25	=	?	+	13

	A	B	C	D	E
	7	9	11	12	13

9	21	÷	3	=	91	÷	?

Test 16 Answer Sheet

	A	B	C	D	E
1	Ⓐ	Ⓑ	Ⓒ	Ⓓ	Ⓔ
2	Ⓐ	Ⓑ	Ⓒ	Ⓓ	Ⓔ
3	Ⓐ	Ⓑ	Ⓒ	Ⓓ	Ⓔ
4	Ⓐ	Ⓑ	Ⓒ	Ⓓ	Ⓔ
5	Ⓐ	Ⓑ	Ⓒ	Ⓓ	Ⓔ
6	Ⓐ	Ⓑ	Ⓒ	Ⓓ	Ⓔ
7	Ⓐ	Ⓑ	Ⓒ	Ⓓ	Ⓔ
8	Ⓐ	Ⓑ	Ⓒ	Ⓓ	Ⓔ
9	Ⓐ	Ⓑ	Ⓒ	Ⓓ	Ⓔ

Test 17 Working with Numbers

This test is given to applicants for jobs in production or technical areas. It's designed to test basic maths skills in a technical context.

Instructions: In this test you are given information about the stock levels of various components. From the five answers given, you must choose the number which should replace the question mark, and blacken the correct circle A, B, C, D, or E on your answer sheet.

Time guideline: there is no official time limit for this test, however try to complete the questions in under 2 minutes.

	COMPONENT	STOCK AT START OF DAY	TOTAL DAILY USAGE	STOCK AT END OF DAY
1		100	?	40

A	B	C	D	E
20	40	60	80	100

	COMPONENT	USAGE (PER HOUR)	WORKING HOURS REMAINING	COMPONENTS REQUIRED
2		5	4	?

A	B	C	D	E
16	1	9	25	20

3	COMPONENT	STOCK AT TIME OF CHECK	USAGE (PER HOUR)	WORKING HOURS REMAINING	STOCK AT END OF DAY
		65	?	2	5

A	B	C	D	E
10	30	72	45	20

Test 17 Answer Sheet

	A	B	C	D	E
1	Ⓐ	Ⓑ	Ⓒ	Ⓓ	Ⓔ
2	Ⓐ	Ⓑ	Ⓒ	Ⓓ	Ⓔ
3	Ⓐ	Ⓑ	Ⓒ	Ⓓ	Ⓔ

Test 18 Using Information

This test measures your ability to understand and use numerical data given in a table. It is used in the selection of individuals in practically oriented jobs such as apprentices and skilled operatives, and for any job where quick and accurate calculations are required.

Instructions: In this test you will need to refer to a timetable and a route map in order to answer questions, each of which takes the form of a passenger enquiry. For each question you are given both the name of the station where you are and the current time. This information will be different in each question, so you must check it carefully.

For each question you must decide which of the five answers given is the correct answer to the enquiry and fill in completely the appropriate circle A, B, C, D or E on your answer sheet.

Now work through the 3 questions below using the timetable and route map.

Time guideline: There is no official time limit for this test, however try to complete the questions in 3 minutes.

Timetable

Milson line							
Brook Road	1730	1745	1755	1802	1805	1811	1815
Appletree Farm	1735	1750	1800	1807	1810	1816	1820
Queens Junction	1739	1754	1804	1811	1814	1820	1824
The Dales	1742	1757	1807	1814	1817	1823	1827
Sinclair Road	1747	1802	1812	1819	1822	1828	1832
Mill Rise	1751	1806	1816	1823	1826	1832	1836

Route map

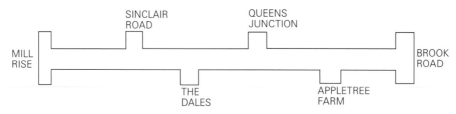

Questions

1	Station: Brook Road Time: 1735	A	B	C	D	E
	When is the next train to Appletree Farm?	1737	1740	1745	1750	1755

2	Station: Queens Junction Time: 1811	A	B	C	D	E
	How long does the train take to reach Sinclair Road?	3 mins	5 mins	6 mins	7 mins	8 mins

3	Station: Appletree Farm Time: 1745	A	B	C	D	E
	How long do I have to wait for the next train to Mill Rise?	5 mins	7 mins	9 mins	10 mins	12 mins

Test 18 Answer Sheet

	A	B	C	D	E
1	Ⓐ	Ⓑ	Ⓒ	Ⓓ	Ⓔ
2	Ⓐ	Ⓑ	Ⓒ	Ⓓ	Ⓔ
3	Ⓐ	Ⓑ	Ⓒ	Ⓓ	Ⓔ

Test 19 Numerical Reasoning

In this test you are given numerical problems to solve. Your ability to reason with numbers is being measured. The test is designed for the selection of clerical and administrative staff of all types. For some tests of this nature you may be allowed to use a calculator, for others you may not.

Instructions: For each question you must choose the correct answer from five possible answers. Indicate your answer by filling in completely the appropriate circle on the answer sheet. *You may use a calculator.*

Time guideline: There are 8 questions – see how many you can do in 3 minutes *using a calculator, or 5 minutes without a calculator.*
Remember to work accurately as well as quickly.

1	If a box of pens costs £7.23, how much would 4 boxes cost?				
	A	B	C	D	E
	£26.46	£26.92	£28.46	£28.82	£28.92

2	What change is due from £5 when purchasing a folder priced at £2.97?				
	A	B	C	D	E
	£1.03	£2.03	£2.13	£3.03	£3.13

3	If 4 pads of paper weigh 0.6kg, what would 7 pads weigh?				
	A	B	C	D	E
	0.15kg	1.05kg	1.10kg	1.15kg	1.5g

4	If I work from 7.45am to 3.30pm Monday to Friday, how many hours do I work in a week?				
	A	B	C	D	E
	37hrs 30mins	37hrs 45mins	38hrs 15mins	38hrs 30mins	38hrs 45mins

5	A part-time office clerk earning £85 per week received a salary increase of 7%. What was the clerk's new salary?				
	A	B	C	D	E
	£90.95	£91.95	£92.00	£92.95	£93

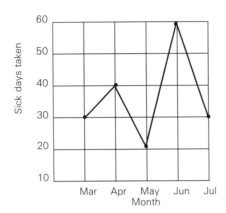

6	From the graph, how many sick days were taken in total during May and June?				
	A	B	C	D	E
	30	40	50	80	70

7	From the graph, what is the average (mean) number of sick days taken between March and July inclusive?				
	A	B	C	D	E
	20	25	36	30	40

8	What percentage of £125 is £25?				
	A	B	C	D	E
	12½%	15%	17½%	20%	22½%

Test 19 Answer Sheet

	A	B	C	D	E
1	Ⓐ	Ⓑ	Ⓒ	Ⓓ	Ⓔ
2	Ⓐ	Ⓑ	Ⓒ	Ⓓ	Ⓔ
3	Ⓐ	Ⓑ	Ⓒ	Ⓓ	Ⓔ
4	Ⓐ	Ⓑ	Ⓒ	Ⓓ	Ⓔ
5	Ⓐ	Ⓑ	Ⓒ	Ⓓ	Ⓔ
6	Ⓐ	Ⓑ	Ⓒ	Ⓓ	Ⓔ
7	Ⓐ	Ⓑ	Ⓒ	Ⓓ	Ⓔ
8	Ⓐ	Ⓑ	Ⓒ	Ⓓ	Ⓔ

Test 20 Numerical Reasoning

In this test you are given numerical problems to solve. All the questions have a technical bias, and can be used in the selection and development of individuals in technically or practically orientated jobs such as craft apprentices, skilled operatives and technical supervisors, or any job in a technical field which involves an element of figure work or calculation.

Instructions: For each question you must choose the correct answer from five possible answers. Indicate your answer by filling in completely the appropriate circle on the answer sheet. *You may use a calculator.*

Time guideline: There are 6 questions – see how many you can do in 3 minutes using a calculator. Remember to work accurately as well as quickly.

1 | If 1,000 ball bearings cost £42.50, how much would 2,300 cost?

A	B	C	D	E
£85	£97.75	£105.50	£110.25	£125.50

2 | How many rivets are needed to attach a 10cm brass plate if one rivet is inserted every 4mm? (10mm = 1cm)

A	B	C	D	E
5	15	25	250	500

3 | When totally full, a barrel contains 75 litres of oil. How many litres of oil remain if 40% has been used?

A	B	C	D	E
1.25 litres	30 litres	45 litres	60 litres	75 litres

4 | A press stamps out 5 components every minute. How many components would be cut out in 8 hours if the same rate was maintained?

A	B	C	D	E
96	300	600	2,400	5,760

5 | What is the area of the steel plate shown below?

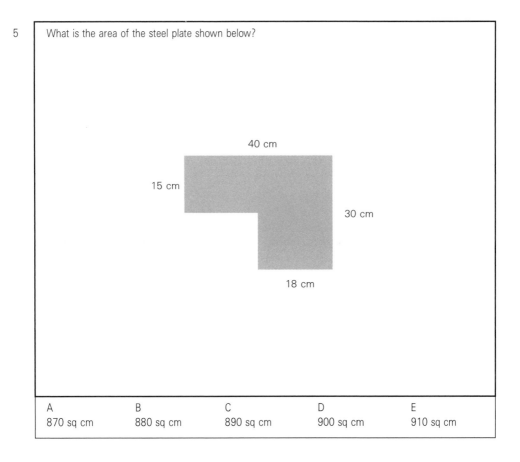

40 cm

15 cm

30 cm

18 cm

A	B	C	D	E
870 sq cm	880 sq cm	890 sq cm	900 sq cm	910 sq cm

6 | A piece of timber has been cut into two lengths in the ratio of 7:2. If the original piece of timber was 828 cm long, how long is the larger of the cut lengths?

A	B	C	D	E
118 cm	184 cm	591 cm	600 cm	644 cm

Test 20 Answer Sheet

	A	B	C	D	E
1	Ⓐ	Ⓑ	Ⓒ	Ⓓ	Ⓔ
2	Ⓐ	Ⓑ	Ⓒ	Ⓓ	Ⓔ
3	Ⓐ	Ⓑ	Ⓒ	Ⓓ	Ⓔ
4	Ⓐ	Ⓑ	Ⓒ	Ⓓ	Ⓔ
5	Ⓐ	Ⓑ	Ⓒ	Ⓓ	Ⓔ
6	Ⓐ	Ⓑ	Ⓒ	Ⓓ	Ⓔ

Test 21 Number Series

The following problems are presented as sequences. They measure your ability to reason with numbers. In particular, this test assesses your ability to develop strategies and to recognise the relationships between numbers. Some of the questions are straightforward, others are a little more complicated.

This type of test is designed for the selection, development and promotion of staff working in Information Technology, for example, software engineers, systems analysts, programmers and database administrators, and for any IT job where the recognition of numerical relationships or sequences is important.

Instructions: Each problem in the test consists of a series of numbers on the left of the page, which follow a logical sequence. You are required to choose the next number in the series from the five options on the right. Indicate your answer by filling in completely the appropriate circles on the answer sheet. *Do not use a calculator.*

Time guideline: See how many questions you can answer in 5 minutes. Remember to work accurately as well as quickly.

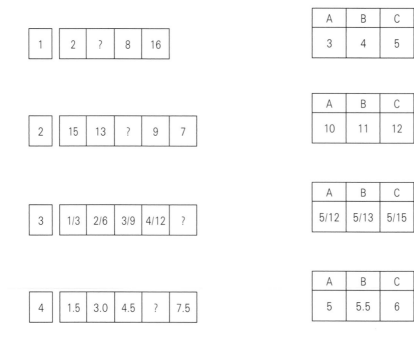

	2	?	8	16
1				

A	B	C	D	E
3	4	5	6	7

	15	13	?	9	7
2					

A	B	C	D	E
10	11	12	13	14

	1/3	2/6	3/9	4/12	?
3					

A	B	C	D	E
5/12	5/13	5/15	6/15	6/16

	1.5	3.0	4.5	?	7.5
4					

A	B	C	D	E
5	5.5	6	6.5	7

5 | 3 | 4 | 5 | 7 | ?

A	B	C	D	E
9	10	11	12	13

6 | ? | 14 | 12 | 11 | 11

A	B	C	D	E
13	15	16	17	28

7 | 4 | 10 | 18 | ? | 40

A	B	C	D	E
28	30	32	34	36

8 | 2 | 4 | 8 | 10 | 20 | ?

A	B	C	D	E
22	24	28	36	40

9 | 2 | 3 | 5 | 8 | ? | 21

A	B	C	D	E
9	11	13	15	17

10 | 2 | 3 | 1 | 4 | 0 | 5 | ?

A	B	C	D	E
– 1	0	1	2	3

Test 21 Answer Sheet

	A	B	C	D	E
1	Ⓐ	Ⓑ	Ⓒ	Ⓓ	Ⓔ
2	Ⓐ	Ⓑ	Ⓒ	Ⓓ	Ⓔ
3	Ⓐ	Ⓑ	Ⓒ	Ⓓ	Ⓔ
4	Ⓐ	Ⓑ	Ⓒ	Ⓓ	Ⓔ
5	Ⓐ	Ⓑ	Ⓒ	Ⓓ	Ⓔ
6	Ⓐ	Ⓑ	Ⓒ	Ⓓ	Ⓔ
7	Ⓐ	Ⓑ	Ⓒ	Ⓓ	Ⓔ
8	Ⓐ	Ⓑ	Ⓒ	Ⓓ	Ⓔ
9	Ⓐ	Ⓑ	Ⓒ	Ⓓ	Ⓔ
10	Ⓐ	Ⓑ	Ⓒ	Ⓓ	Ⓔ

Test 22 Numerical Estimation

In this test your ability to quickly *estimate* the answer to a calculation is being assessed. When you take a test of this type, you will not have sufficient time to calculate the exact answer. This skill is very useful in the automated office environment where calculations made by computers often need to be cross-checked in case of errors in data input.

This type of test is often used in the selection of school leavers and work-experienced applicants, at both clerical and supervisory level, and by a variety of organisations including building societies, banks, retailers and many public sector organisations. Types of job include accounts clerks, clerical supervisors, mail order clerks and positions where VDUs or automated equipment will be used.

Instructions: In this test you are required to *estimate* the order of magnitude of the solution to each calculation and then choose the answer which is nearest to your estimate from the 5 alternative answers.

Indicate your answers by filling in completely the appropriate boxes on the answer sheet. *Do not use a calculator.*

Time guideline: There is no official time guideline for this practice test. However, because in a real live test situation you will not be given sufficient time to calculate the exact answer, work as quickly as you possibly can.

1    $19 + 27$

A	B	C	D	E
56	32	46	4.6	306

2   20% of 56

A	B	C	D	E
280	11.2	28	112	2.8

3    $72 - 18$

A	B	C	D	E
660	64	540	54	66

4   24×12

A	B	C	D	E
288	48	306	36	28.8

Test 22 Answer Sheet

1   Ⓐ   Ⓑ   Ⓒ   Ⓓ   Ⓔ
2   Ⓐ   Ⓑ   Ⓒ   Ⓓ   Ⓔ
3   Ⓐ   Ⓑ   Ⓒ   Ⓓ   Ⓔ
4   Ⓐ   Ⓑ   Ⓒ   Ⓓ   Ⓔ

Test 23 Numerical Estimation

Now try another numerical estimation test. It also measures your ability to quickly estimate the answers to numerical calculations.

This type of test is often used in the selection of qualified school leavers for modern apprenticeship schemes, or for graduates and work-experienced personnel moving into applied technology areas. It can be used to select candidates for jobs such as electronics and electrical technicians, research technicians and many other technically orientated jobs.

Instructions: This test is a short one with only two questions. As in the previous test, you must *estimate* the answers, and then choose the answer which is nearest to your estimate from the 5 alternative answers. You will be discouraged from making precise calculations by a time constraint.

Indicate your answers by filling in completely the appropriate circles on the answer sheet. *Do not use a calculator.*

Time guideline: There is no official time guideline for this practice test. However, because in a real live test situation you will not be given sufficient time to calculate the exact answer, work as quickly as you possibly can.

1

24 × 0.8 = ?	A	B	C	D	E
	16	220	19	24	140

2

76% of 156 = ?	A	B	C	D	E
	120	160	140	100	180

Test 23 Answer Sheet

	A	B	C	D	E
1	Ⓐ	Ⓑ	Ⓒ	Ⓓ	Ⓔ
2	Ⓐ	Ⓑ	Ⓒ	Ⓓ	Ⓔ

Test 24 Interpreting Data

This test measures your ability to understand facts and figures in statistical tables and make logical deductions from the given information. Certainly, the ability to interpret data from a variety of different sources such as tables, graphs and charts is a common requirement in many managerial and professional jobs.

This type of test is often used to select candidates for administrative and supervisory jobs, as well as junior managers and management trainees, and any job involving analysis or decision-making based on numerical facts.

Instructions: For each question, indicate your answer by filling in completely the appropriate circle on the answer sheet. *Do not use a calculator. You may use rough paper for your workings-out.*

Time guideline: There is no official time guideline for this practice test, however, try to work through the questions as quickly as you can. Remember that accuracy is equally important.

Newspaper Readership				
	Readership (millions)		Percentage of Adults Reading each Paper in 1990	
Daily Newspapers	1981	1990	Males	Females
The Daily Chronicle	3.6	2.9	7	6
Daily News	13.8	9.3	24	18
The Tribune	1.1	1.4	4	3
The Herald	8.5	12.7	30	23
Daily Echo	4.8	4.9	10	12

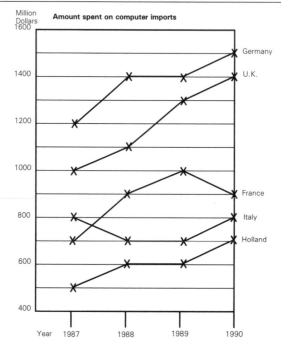

Interpreting Data – Questions

1 Which newspaper was read by a higher percentage of females than males in 1990?

A	B	C	D	E
The Tribune	The Herald	Daily News	Daily Echo	The Daily Chronicle

2 In 1989, how much more than Italy did Germany spend on computer imports?

A	B	C	D	E
650 million	700 million	750 million	800 million	850 million

3 What was the combined readership of the Daily Chronicle, Echo and Tribune in 1981?

A	B	C	D	E
10.6	8.4	9.5	12.2	7.8

4 If the amount spent on computer imports into the U.K. in 1991 was 20% lower than in 1990, what was spent in 1991?

A	B	C	D	E
1080	1120	1160	1220	1300

5 Which newspaper showed the largest change in female readership between 1981 and 1990?

A	B	C	D	E
Daily Echo	The Tribune	The Herald	The Daily Chronicle	Cannot Say

6 Which countries experienced a drop in the value of computers imported from one year to the next?

A	B	C	D	E
France & Italy	France & Holland	Holland & Italy	U.K. & Holland	Italy & U.K.

Test 24 Answer Sheet

	A	B	C	D	E
1	Ⓐ	Ⓑ	Ⓒ	Ⓓ	Ⓔ
2	Ⓐ	Ⓑ	Ⓒ	Ⓓ	Ⓔ
3	Ⓐ	Ⓑ	Ⓒ	Ⓓ	Ⓔ
4	Ⓐ	Ⓑ	Ⓒ	Ⓓ	Ⓔ
5	Ⓐ	Ⓑ	Ⓒ	Ⓓ	Ⓔ
6	Ⓐ	Ⓑ	Ⓒ	Ⓓ	Ⓔ

Test 25 Numerical Evaluation

This test measures your ability to evaluate or make deductions from complex numerical data laid out in the form of tables, graphs or charts. This type of test is often used in the selection and development of individuals over a wide range of sales or customer service roles.

Instructions: Look at the facts and figures presented in the various tables. In each question you are given five answers to choose from. One, and only one of the answers is correct in each case. Indicate your answer by filling in completely the appropriate circle on the answer sheet. *You may use a calculator.*

Time guideline: See how many questions you can answer in 5 minutes.

	INTERNATIONAL PRODUCT SALES (Sales Revenue £ 000's)			
	Europe		North America	
Product Stock Codes	Last Year	This Year	Last Year	This Year
A002	17	31	410	354
B008	26	56	18	59
C015	21	69	27	71
D024	37	67	13	50
E001	31	32	19	37
F073	36	16	29	19

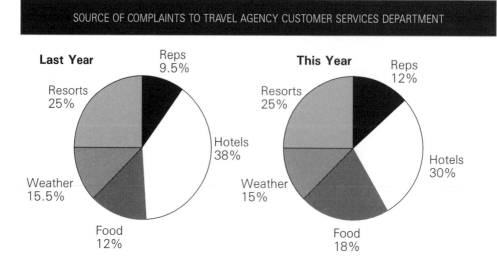

SOURCE OF COMPLAINTS TO TRAVEL AGENCY CUSTOMER SERVICES DEPARTMENT

Last Year
Reps 9.5%
Resorts 25%
Hotels 38%
Weather 15.5%
Food 12%

This Year
Reps 12%
Resorts 25%
Hotels 30%
Weather 15%
Food 18%

1   Of the following, which had the highest sales revenue last year?

A	B	C	D	E
B008 in Europe	D024 in N America	E001 in Europe	C015 in N America	F073 in Europe

2   This year, which two sources together attracted more than half the complaints received?

A	B	C	D	E
Reps and Resorts	Food and Hotels	Hotels and Resorts	Resorts and Weather	Resorts and Food

3   If product E001 was sold at a price of £44.80 per unit this year, approximately how many units were sold in North America this year?

A	B	C	D	E
826	1,250	1,272	2,656	2,509

4   If last year, 'resorts' generated 600 complaints, how many complaints did 'hotels' generate?

A	B	C	D	E
900	912	930	945	968

5   If 'food' generated 330 complaints this year, representing an **increase** of 10% from last year, approximately how many complaints were there about 'weather' last year?

A	B	C	D	E
300	388	474	1833	2500

6   What was the approximate % increase in revenue generated by European sales of D024 from last year to this?

A	B	C	D	E
45%	55%	76%	81%	92%

Test 25 Answer Sheet

	A	B	C	D	E
1	Ⓐ	Ⓑ	Ⓒ	Ⓓ	Ⓔ
2	Ⓐ	Ⓑ	Ⓒ	Ⓓ	Ⓔ
3	Ⓐ	Ⓑ	Ⓒ	Ⓓ	Ⓔ
4	Ⓐ	Ⓑ	Ⓒ	Ⓓ	Ⓔ
5	Ⓐ	Ⓑ	Ⓒ	Ⓓ	Ⓔ
6	Ⓐ	Ⓑ	Ⓒ	Ⓓ	Ⓔ

Test 26 Numerical Test

This test measures your ability to understand facts and figures in statistical tables and make logical deductions from the given information. The ability to interpret data from a variety of different sources such as tables, graphs and charts is a common requirement in many managerial and professional jobs.

This type of test is used in the selection of graduates, managers and supervisors over a wide range of industries.

Instructions: For each question you are given either five or ten options from which to choose. One, and only one of the answers is correct in each case. Indicate your answer by filling in completely the appropriate circle on the answer sheet. Please note that for questions which have 10 options you may have to fill in more than one circle to indicate your answer. *Some organisations allow the use of a calculator for this test, others do not. Therefore I suggest you try to manage without.*

Time guideline: There is no official time guideline, however work as quickly as you can. *You may use rough paper for your workings-out.*

Statistical tables

Population Structure 1985

	Population at start of year (millions)	Live Births per 1,000 population (Jan-Dec)	Deaths per 1,000 population (Jan-Dec)	Percentage of population at start of year aged under 15	60 or over
UK	56.6	13.3	11.8	19	21
France	55.2	13.9	10.0	21	19
Italy	57.1	10.1	9.5	19	19
West Germany	61.0	9.6	11.5	15	20
Spain	38.6	12.1	7.7	23	17

Production of 15mm Buttons, July–December

Sales price standard quality buttons – £5.70 per 100.
Sales price sub-standard buttons – £2.85 per 100.

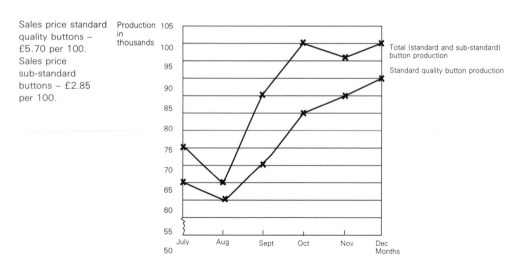

Total (standard and sub-standard) button production

Standard quality button production

1   Which country had the highest number of people aged 60 or over at the start of 1985?

A	B	C	D	E
UK	France	Italy	W. Germany	Spain

2   What percentage of the total 15mm button production was classed as sub-standard in September?

A	B	C	D	E
10.5%	13%	15%	17.5%	20%
AB	AC	AD	AE	BC
23.5%	25%	27.5%	28%	30.5%

3   How many live births occurred in 1985 in Spain and Italy together (to the nearest 1,000)?

A	B	C	D	E
104,000	840,000	1,044,000	8,400,000	10,440,000

4   What was the net effect on the UK population of the live birth and death rates in 1985?

A	B	C	D	E
Decrease of 66,700	Increase of 84,900	Increase of 85,270	Increase of 742,780	Cannot say

5   By how much did the total sales value of November's button production vary from October's?

A	B	C	D	E
£28.50 (Decrease)	£142.40 (Decrease)	£285.00 (Increase)	£427.50 (Decrease)	No change

6   What was the loss in potential sales revenue attributable to the production of sub-standard (as opposed to standard) buttons over the 6 month period?

A	B	C	D	E
£213.75	£427.50	£2,137.50	£2,280.00	£4,275.00

Test 26 Answer Sheet

	A	B	C	D	E
1	Ⓐ	Ⓑ	Ⓒ	Ⓓ	Ⓔ
2	Ⓐ	Ⓑ	Ⓒ	Ⓓ	Ⓔ
3	Ⓐ	Ⓑ	Ⓒ	Ⓓ	Ⓔ
4	Ⓐ	Ⓑ	Ⓒ	Ⓓ	Ⓔ
5	Ⓐ	Ⓑ	Ⓒ	Ⓓ	Ⓔ
6	Ⓐ	Ⓑ	Ⓒ	Ⓓ	Ⓔ

Test 27 Numerical Interpretation

In this test you will be using facts and figures presented in various tables to answer questions designed to assess your ability to reason with data – a common requirement of many managerial and professional jobs. This type of test is often used to select candidates for jobs in sales and customer contact areas at supervisory and junior management level, and for jobs involving analysis or decision-making based on numerical facts.

Instructions: Using the information in the table and pie chart, answer each question by filling in completely the appropriate circle on the answer sheet. Remember that each question has one, and only one, correct answer. *You may use a calculator.*

Time guideline: See how many questions you can answer in 5 minutes.

TELEPHONE CALLS RECEIVED BY CUSTOMER SERVICES THIS MONTH				
Person taking call	Number of product enquiries	Number of complaints	Number of accounts queries	Total number of calls
Jo	155	6	6	167
Mark	310	2	10	322
Michelle	205	0	47	252
Susan	112	14	25	151
Tony	370	8	35	413

COST OF PROMOTIONAL ACTIVITIES IN LAST FINANCIAL YEAR

Total cost over year: £80,000

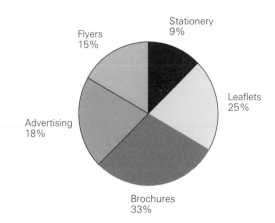

1 How many product enquiries were received this month?

A	B	C	D	E
1,142	1,152	1,182	1,232	1,292

2 If each complaint call lasted for an average of 12 mins, how much time was spent dealing with complaint calls?

A	B	C	D	E
5 hours 12 mins	5 hours 24 mins	5 hours 36 mins	5 hours 48 mins	6 hours

3 Two-thirds of complaining customers received a £15 voucher and the rest received a £50 voucher. What was the total value of these vouchers?

A	B	C	D	E
£500	£760	£800	£1,010	£1,150

4 How much money was spent on promotional stationery in the last financial year?

A	B	C	D	E
£4,900	£5,300	£6,800	£7,200	£7,400

5 If 50,000 brochures were printed, what was the approximate cost per brochure?

A	B	C	D	E
26p	44p	53p	62p	78p

6 If the average cost of printing a flyer is 4p, how many were printed in the last financial year?

A	B	C	D	E
200,000	300,000	400,000	600,000	900,000

Test 27 Answer Sheet

	A	B	C	D	E
1	Ⓐ	Ⓑ	Ⓒ	Ⓓ	Ⓔ
2	Ⓐ	Ⓑ	Ⓒ	Ⓓ	Ⓔ
3	Ⓐ	Ⓑ	Ⓒ	Ⓓ	Ⓔ
4	Ⓐ	Ⓑ	Ⓒ	Ⓓ	Ⓔ
5	Ⓐ	Ⓑ	Ⓒ	Ⓓ	Ⓔ
6	Ⓐ	Ⓑ	Ⓒ	Ⓓ	Ⓔ

Test 28 Interpreting Numerical Data

The ability to interpret, analyse and evaluate numerical or statistical data is a common requirement for many types of jobs, especially those involving any decision-making based on numerical facts.

Instructions: In this test you will be using facts and figures presented in a diagram to answer a range of questions. In each question you are given five alternative answers to choose from. Fill in completely the appropriate circle on the answer sheet. One and only one of the alternatives is correct in each case.
    You may use rough paper and a pencil for working out your answers, but *not a calculator.*

Time guideline: Try to answer all the questions in 4 minutes.

Full-time employment destinations of women leaving university

TOTAL = 6,500

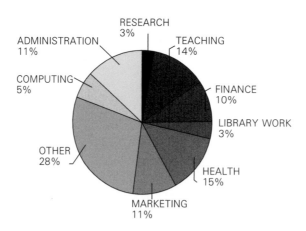

1   What percentage of women leaving university went into finance and administration?

A	B	C	D	E
11%	19%	22%	21%	31%

2   Which one area of employment is least popular with female university leavers?

A	B	C	D	E
Computing	Library Work	Marketing	Research	Cannot say

3 Which area of work was most frequently chosen by women leaving university?

A	B	C	D	E
Administration	Finance	Health	Sales	Teaching

4 Into which two areas of employment did a combined 19% of female university leavers go?

A	B	C	D	E
Administration and Computing	Health and Research	Marketing and Administration	Teaching and Computing	Teaching and Library

5 How many women went into teaching when they left university?

A	B	C	D	E
140	650	870	910	None of these

6 How many more women went into computing than research?

A	B	C	D	E
120	135	195	325	None of these

7 How many women went into computing and administration?

A	B	C	D	E
940	1,040	1,100	1,140	None of these

8 24% of female university leavers go into ...

A	B	C	D	E
Finance, Research and Administration	Finance, Teaching and Research	Health, Computing and Research	Marketing, Finance and Computing	Teaching, Research and Administration

Test 28 Answer Sheet

	A	B	C	D	E
1	Ⓐ	Ⓑ	Ⓒ	Ⓓ	Ⓔ
2	Ⓐ	Ⓑ	Ⓒ	Ⓓ	Ⓔ
3	Ⓐ	Ⓑ	Ⓒ	Ⓓ	Ⓔ
4	Ⓐ	Ⓑ	Ⓒ	Ⓓ	Ⓔ
5	Ⓐ	Ⓑ	Ⓒ	Ⓓ	Ⓔ
6	Ⓐ	Ⓑ	Ⓒ	Ⓓ	Ⓔ
7	Ⓐ	Ⓑ	Ⓒ	Ⓓ	Ⓔ
8	Ⓐ	Ⓑ	Ⓒ	Ⓓ	Ⓔ

Test 29 Interpreting Numerical Data

The ability to interpret, analyse and evaluate numerical or statistical data is a common requirement for many types of jobs, especially those involving any decision-making based on numerical facts.

Instructions: In this test you will be using facts and figures presented in a graph to answer a range of questions. In each question you are given five alternative answers to choose from. Fill in completely the appropriate circle on the answer sheet. One and only one of the alternatives is correct in each case.
You may use rough paper and a pencil for working out your answers, but *not a calculator*.

Time guideline: Try to answer all the questions in 4 minutes.

Merchandise, coal and liquid lifted (carried) by inland waterways

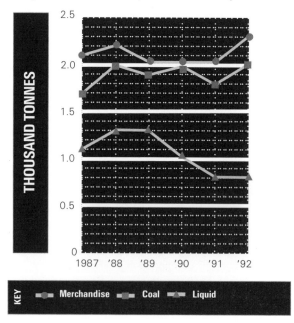

1   How many thousand tonnes of liquids were lifted in 1989?

A	B	C	D	E
1.3	1.5	1.9	2.00	None of these

2   How much more coal was lifted in 1992 than in 1987? (Answer choices are given in thousand tonnes.)

A	B	C	D	E
0.1	0.2	0.3	1.3	2.0

3   How many thousand tonnes of merchandise and liquids were lifted in 1991?

A	B	C	D	E
2.2	2.8	2.9	3.00	1.9

4   In which year was most merchandise carried?

A	B	C	D	E
1988	1990	1991	1992	1989

5   In 1988 how much more merchandise than liquids was lifted? (Answer choices are given in thousand tonnes.)

A	B	C	D	E
0.2	0.9	1.00	1.1	2.2

6   How much more liquid was carried in 1989 than in 1992? (Answer choices are given in thousand tonnes.)

A	B	C	D	E
0.5	0.8	1.3	1.5	1.8

7   In which year was an equal tonnage of merchandise and coal carried?

A	B	C	D	E
1987	1988	1990	1991	1992

Test 29 Answer Sheet

	A	B	C	D	E
1	Ⓐ	Ⓑ	Ⓒ	Ⓓ	Ⓔ
2	Ⓐ	Ⓑ	Ⓒ	Ⓓ	Ⓔ
3	Ⓐ	Ⓑ	Ⓒ	Ⓓ	Ⓔ
4	Ⓐ	Ⓑ	Ⓒ	Ⓓ	Ⓔ
5	Ⓐ	Ⓑ	Ⓒ	Ⓓ	Ⓔ
6	Ⓐ	Ⓑ	Ⓒ	Ⓓ	Ⓔ
7	Ⓐ	Ⓑ	Ⓒ	Ⓓ	Ⓔ

Test 30 Interpreting Numerical Data

The ability to interpret, analyse and evaluate numerical or statistical data is a common requirement for many types of jobs, especially those involving any decision-making based on numerical facts.

Instructions: In this test you will be using facts and figures presented in a table to answer a range of questions. In each question you are given five alternative answers to choose from. Fill in completely the appropriate circle on the answer sheet. One and only one of the alternatives is correct in each case.
    You may use rough paper and a pencil for working out your answers, but *not a calculator.*

Time guideline: Try to answer all the questions in 4 minutes.

Expenditure per pupil (£)

	PRIMARY SCHOOLS	
	London Authorities	**Other Authorities**
Staff	774	565
Premises	134	85
Books and equipment	34	21
Other	6	7

	SECONDARY SCHOOLS	
	London Authorities	**Other Authorities**
Staff	1088	797
Premises	184	137
Books and equipment	61	36
Other	24	15

1   How much more per pupil do London authorities spend on staff in secondary schools than in primary schools?

A	B	C	D	E
£209	£219	£232	£291	£314

2   How much more than 'other' authorities do London authorities spend per secondary pupil on premises?

A	B	C	D	E
£39	£47	£184	£137	£291

3   What is the total cost to London authorities per secondary school pupil?

A	B	C	D	E
£688	£948	£985	£1,357	£1,427

4   On what do 'other' authorities spend 13.8% of their total outlay per primary school pupil?

A	B	C	D	E
Books and Equipment	Premises	Staff	Other	Cannot say

5   What is the total expenditure for a primary school in London with 320 pupils?

A	B	C	D	E
£300,360	£303,360	£330,306	£330,360	£360,303

6   What is the difference in total cost to London authorities between one secondary pupil and one primary pupil?

A	B	C	D	E
£260	£314	£409	£948	None of these

7   Approximately what proportion of the total amount spent per primary pupil by 'other' authorities is on books and equipment?

A	B	C	D	E
1%	3%	10%	12%	17%

Test 30 Answer Sheet

	A	B	C	D	E
1	Ⓐ	Ⓑ	Ⓒ	Ⓓ	Ⓔ
2	Ⓐ	Ⓑ	Ⓒ	Ⓓ	Ⓔ
3	Ⓐ	Ⓑ	Ⓒ	Ⓓ	Ⓔ
4	Ⓐ	Ⓑ	Ⓒ	Ⓓ	Ⓔ
5	Ⓐ	Ⓑ	Ⓒ	Ⓓ	Ⓔ
6	Ⓐ	Ⓑ	Ⓒ	Ⓓ	Ⓔ
7	Ⓐ	Ⓑ	Ⓒ	Ⓓ	Ⓔ

Answers to Numerical Reasoning questions

Test 14 Number Skills

	A	B	C	D
1	A	●	C	D
2	A	B	●	D
3	A	B	C	●

Test 15 Numerical Computation

	A	B	C	D	E
1	A	B	C	●	E
2	●	B	C	D	E
3	A	B	●	D	E
4	A	B	C	D	●
5	A	B	●	D	E
6	A	●	C	D	E
7	●	B	C	D	E
8	A	●	C	D	E
9	A	B	C	●	E
10	A	B	C	●	E

Test 16 Numerical Computation

	A	B	C	D	E
1	A	●	C	D	E
2	A	B	●	D	E
3	A	B	C	D	●
4	A	B	C	●	E
5	A	B	●	D	E
6	A	B	C	●	E
7	A	B	C	D	●
8	●	B	C	D	E
9	A	B	C	D	●

Test 17 Working with Numbers

	A	B	C	D	E
1	A	B	●	D	E
2	A	B	C	D	●
3	A	●	C	D	E

Test 18 Using Information

	A	B	C	D	E
1	A	B	●	D	E
2	A	B	C	D	●
3	●	B	C	D	E

Test 19 Numerical Reasoning

	A	B	C	D	E
1	A	B	C	D	●
2	A	●	C	D	E
3	A	●	C	D	E
4	A	B	C	D	●
5	●	B	C	D	E
6	A	B	C	●	E
7	A	B	●	D	E
8	A	B	C	●	E

Test 20 Numerical Reasoning

	A	B	C	D	E
1	A	●	C	D	E
2	A	B	●	D	E
3	A	B	●	D	E
4	A	B	C	●	E
5	●	B	C	D	E
6	A	B	C	D	●

Test 21 Number Series

	A	B	C	D	E
1	A	●	C	D	E
2	A	●	C	D	E
3	A	B	●	D	E
4	A	B	●	D	E
5	●	B	C	D	E
6	A	B	C	●	E
7	●	B	C	D	E
8	●	B	C	D	E
9	A	B	●	D	E
10	●	B	C	D	E

Test 22 Numerical Estimation

	A	B	C	D	E
1	Ⓐ	Ⓑ	●	Ⓓ	Ⓔ
2	Ⓐ	●	Ⓒ	Ⓓ	Ⓔ
3	Ⓐ	Ⓑ	Ⓒ	●	Ⓔ
4	●	Ⓑ	Ⓒ	Ⓓ	Ⓔ

Test 23 Numerical Estimation

	A	B	C	D	E
1	Ⓐ	Ⓑ	●	Ⓓ	Ⓔ
2	●	Ⓑ	Ⓒ	Ⓓ	Ⓔ

Test 24 Interpreting Data

	A	B	C	D	E
1	Ⓐ	Ⓑ	Ⓒ	●	Ⓔ
2	Ⓐ	●	Ⓒ	Ⓓ	Ⓔ
3	Ⓐ	Ⓑ	●	Ⓓ	Ⓔ
4	Ⓐ	●	Ⓒ	Ⓓ	Ⓔ
5	Ⓐ	Ⓑ	Ⓒ	Ⓓ	●
6	●	Ⓑ	Ⓒ	Ⓓ	Ⓔ

Test 25 Numerical Evaluation

	A	B	C	D	E
1	Ⓐ	Ⓑ	Ⓒ	Ⓓ	●
2	Ⓐ	Ⓑ	●	Ⓓ	Ⓔ
3	●	Ⓑ	Ⓒ	Ⓓ	Ⓔ
4	Ⓐ	●	Ⓒ	Ⓓ	Ⓔ
5	Ⓐ	●	Ⓒ	Ⓓ	Ⓔ
6	Ⓐ	Ⓑ	Ⓒ	●	Ⓔ

Test 26 Numerical Test

	A	B	C	D	E
1	Ⓐ	Ⓑ	Ⓒ	●	Ⓔ
2	●	●	Ⓒ	Ⓓ	Ⓔ
3	Ⓐ	Ⓑ	●	Ⓓ	Ⓔ
4	Ⓐ	●	Ⓒ	Ⓓ	Ⓔ
5	Ⓐ	Ⓑ	Ⓒ	Ⓓ	●
6	Ⓐ	Ⓑ	●	Ⓓ	Ⓔ

Test 27 Numerical Interpretation

	A	B	C	D	E
1	Ⓐ	●	Ⓒ	Ⓓ	Ⓔ
2	Ⓐ	Ⓑ	Ⓒ	Ⓓ	●
3	Ⓐ	Ⓑ	●	Ⓓ	Ⓔ
4	Ⓐ	Ⓑ	Ⓒ	●	Ⓔ
5	Ⓐ	Ⓑ	●	Ⓓ	Ⓔ
6	Ⓐ	●	Ⓒ	Ⓓ	Ⓔ

Test 28 Interpreting Numerical Data

	A	B	C	D	E
1	Ⓐ	Ⓑ	Ⓒ	●	Ⓔ
2	Ⓐ	Ⓑ	Ⓒ	Ⓓ	●
3	Ⓐ	Ⓑ	●	Ⓓ	Ⓔ
4	Ⓐ	Ⓑ	Ⓒ	●	Ⓔ
5	Ⓐ	Ⓑ	Ⓒ	●	Ⓔ
6	Ⓐ	Ⓑ	Ⓒ	Ⓓ	●
7	Ⓐ	●	Ⓒ	Ⓓ	Ⓔ
8	●	Ⓑ	Ⓒ	Ⓓ	Ⓔ

Test 29 Interpreting Numerical Data

	A	B	C	D	E
1	●	Ⓑ	Ⓒ	Ⓓ	Ⓔ
2	Ⓐ	Ⓑ	●	Ⓓ	Ⓔ
3	Ⓐ	●	Ⓒ	Ⓓ	Ⓔ
4	Ⓐ	Ⓑ	Ⓒ	●	Ⓔ
5	Ⓐ	●	Ⓒ	Ⓓ	Ⓔ
6	Ⓐ	Ⓑ	●	Ⓓ	Ⓔ
7	Ⓐ	Ⓑ	●	Ⓓ	Ⓔ

Test 30 Interpreting Numerical Data

	A	B	C	D	E
1	Ⓐ	Ⓑ	Ⓒ	Ⓓ	●
2	Ⓐ	●	Ⓒ	Ⓓ	Ⓔ
3	Ⓐ	Ⓑ	Ⓒ	●	Ⓔ
4	Ⓐ	●	Ⓒ	Ⓓ	Ⓔ
5	Ⓐ	●	Ⓒ	Ⓓ	Ⓔ
6	Ⓐ	Ⓑ	●	Ⓓ	Ⓔ
7	Ⓐ	●	Ⓒ	Ⓓ	Ⓔ

Numerical tests – how to improve your performance

However numerical reasoning questions are presented, and at whatever level, you really do need a sound understanding of the following basic maths skills:

✓ addition
✓ subtraction
✓ multiplication
✓ division
✓ decimal numbers
✓ fractions
✓ percentages.

This is essential, especially for questions which require any sort of mental calculation. Remember that for many numerical reasoning tests, the use of a calculator is prohibited (however, take along a calculator, just in case).

Basic maths skills are all very well, but in higher level tests your ability to *reason* with numbers is also being tested. Here are some ways to improve your numerical reasoning ability:

◆ Learn your times-tables off by heart.

◆ Consider buying yourself a basic maths textbook and do a little bit of revision (there are lots of very good maths sites on the internet too).

◆ Practise maths with and without a calculator. Practising really does make a difference.

◆ Do number puzzles in newspapers and magazines.

◆ Keep score when playing games like darts, card games etc.

◆ Calculate how much your shopping will cost before you reach the till.

◆ Work out how much change you should receive when you pay for something.

◆ Read financial reports in newspapers.

◆ Study tables of data.

♦ Always read the questions themselves very carefully to ensure you understand exactly what it is you are being asked – don't make any assumptions.

♦ Look at the answer choices and quickly eliminate any you know to be incorrect. Concentrate your energies on deciding between the most likely possibilities.

♦ Estimating the solution in your head *before* you look at the answer choices can save you a lot of time and give you confidence that you've chosen correctly.

♦ Numerical reasoning tests demand a high level of concentration and brain work, so treat yourself to a break every now and then. Sit up straight, shut your eyes and take a few deep breaths, just for 20 seconds or so. This will calm you down, relax your back and give your eyes and brain a well deserved rest.

♦ If you really feel that the correct solution is *not* included in the answer choices, take an educated guess and move on. Mistakes on numerical reasoning exam papers do crop up every now and then – occupational psychologists are only human after all!

CHAPTER FIVE

Abstract Reasoning

Abstract reasoning tests, or diagrammatic reasoning tests as they are sometimes called, are psychometric tests which use diagrams, symbols, signs or shapes instead of words and numbers. In other words, they are *visual* questions. And because they require good visual-thinking and logic skills they are often used to select candidates for jobs in the IT industry. However, many employers consider them to be a very good indicator of a person's general intellectual ability and for this reason they are also given to applicants over a very wide range of jobs.

Abstract reasoning tests measure:

- logical analysis
- visual thinking
- the ability to work through complex problems systematically.

When you look at abstract reasoning tests for the first time, they often appear absolutely impossible to figure out, but on closer inspection you'll see they are not that difficult. To solve sequence questions, for example, you just have to look for patterns. Instead of seeing each illustration as a mass of shapes and symbols, try to work out what each separate element inside the illustration is doing as it progresses through the sequence, and therefore what it will do next.

If all else fails, look at the tips at the end of the chapter. You can also try figuring out how the questions work with the answers in front of you, at least until you get the idea.

All abstract reasoning tests are strictly timed, and *every single question will have one, and only one correct answer.*

In this chapter

In this chapter there are five different abstract reasoning tests for you to try. Before each one I've indicated for what sort of job, and for what industry, you might be expected to take that particular type of test.

At the end of this chapter there is section entitled **Abstract Reasoning Tests – How To Improve Your Performance** which is intended to help you do just that across the whole range of abstract reasoning tests. Included in this section are some hints on tackling the questions themselves. If you have a problem with any of the questions then hopefully the advice contained in this section will get you back on track. Remember, however, that all of us have strengths and weaknesses, and everyone will have some difficulty with some of the tests in this book.

Test 31 Diagrammatic Series

The following test measures your ability to recognise logical sequences within a series of diagrams or symbols.

This type of test is often used to assess reasoning skills at administrative, supervisory and junior management levels – in fact any occupation where logical or analytical reasoning is required. It could be used to select applicants for administrative and supervisory jobs, junior managers, management trainees, and jobs involving technical research or computer programming.

Instructions: Each problem in the test consists of a series of diagrams, on the left of the page, which follow a logical sequence. You are required to choose the next diagram in the series from the five options on the right. Indicate your answer by filling in completely the appropriate circle on the answer sheet.

Time guideline: See how many questions you can answer in 5 minutes. Remember to work accurately as well as quickly.

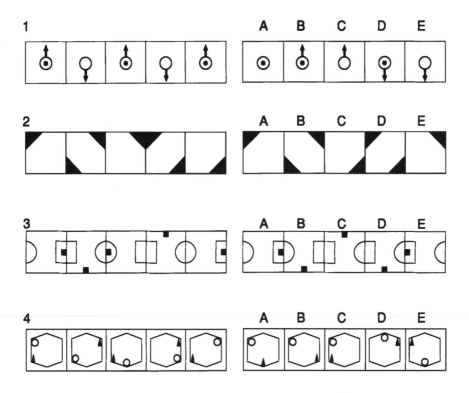

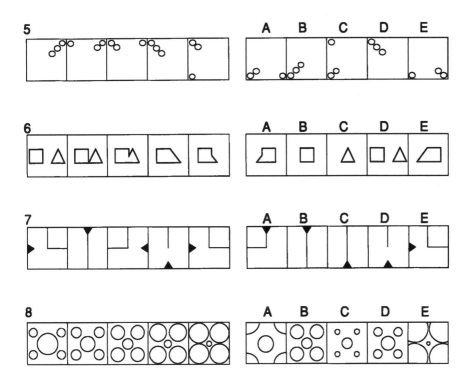

Test 31 Answer Sheet

	A	B	C	D	E
1	Ⓐ	Ⓑ	Ⓒ	Ⓓ	Ⓔ
2	Ⓐ	Ⓑ	Ⓒ	Ⓓ	Ⓔ
3	Ⓐ	Ⓑ	Ⓒ	Ⓓ	Ⓔ
4	Ⓐ	Ⓑ	Ⓒ	Ⓓ	Ⓔ
5	Ⓐ	Ⓑ	Ⓒ	Ⓓ	Ⓔ
6	Ⓐ	Ⓑ	Ⓒ	Ⓓ	Ⓔ
7	Ⓐ	Ⓑ	Ⓒ	Ⓓ	Ⓔ
8	Ⓐ	Ⓑ	Ⓒ	Ⓓ	Ⓔ

Test 32 Diagrammatic Reasoning

This test, which I think is really quite difficult, measures logical and analytical reasoning and requires the recognition of logical rules governing sequences. It is used in the selection of candidates for positions in administration and junior management, for example, office supervisors, senior personal assistants, management trainees, sales and customer service staff, technical research and computer programming. Look at the tips at the end of the chapter if you get stuck.

Instructions: This is a test of reasoning with diagrams. Each problem in this test consists of a series of five diagrams that follow a logical sequence. Your task is to work out which diagram comes next in the series from the five options labelled A–E. Fill in completely the appropriate circle on the answer sheet.

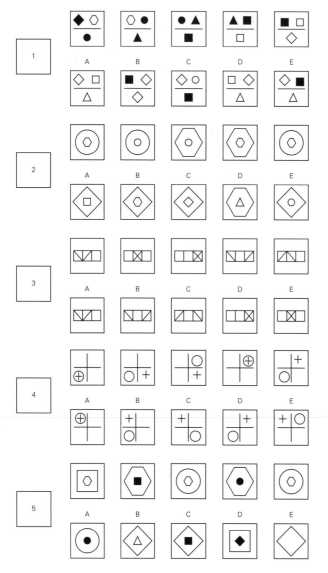

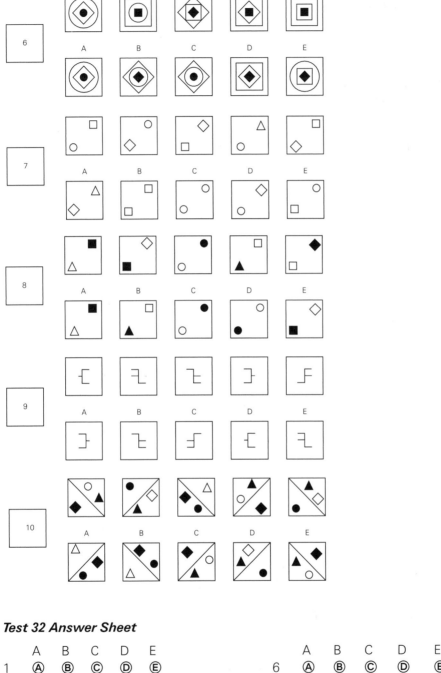

Test 32 Answer Sheet

	A	B	C	D	E			A	B	C	D	E
1	Ⓐ	Ⓑ	Ⓒ	Ⓓ	Ⓔ		6	Ⓐ	Ⓑ	Ⓒ	Ⓓ	Ⓔ
2	Ⓐ	Ⓑ	Ⓒ	Ⓓ	Ⓔ		7	Ⓐ	Ⓑ	Ⓒ	Ⓓ	Ⓔ
3	Ⓐ	Ⓑ	Ⓒ	Ⓓ	Ⓔ		8	Ⓐ	Ⓑ	Ⓒ	Ⓓ	Ⓔ
4	Ⓐ	Ⓑ	Ⓒ	Ⓓ	Ⓔ		9	Ⓐ	Ⓑ	Ⓒ	Ⓓ	Ⓔ
5	Ⓐ	Ⓑ	Ⓒ	Ⓓ	Ⓔ		10	Ⓐ	Ⓑ	Ⓒ	Ⓓ	Ⓔ

Test 33 Diagramming

This abstract reasoning test measures logical analysis through the ability to follow complex instructions. It simulates the ability to handle multiple and independent commands, an important ability in most IT jobs. This type of test is therefore specifically designed for the selection, development and promotion of staff working in the IT industry, for example, software engineers, systems analysts, programmers and database administrators.

Instructions: In this test, figures (shapes) in BOXES are presented in columns. They are changed in various ways by commands represented as symbols in CIRCLES. A complete list of these commands and what they do is shown below. Fill in completely the apporpriate circle on the answer sheet.

Time guideline: See how many questions you can answer in 4 minutes.

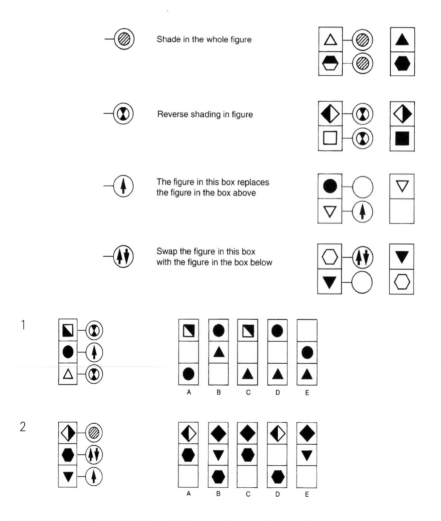

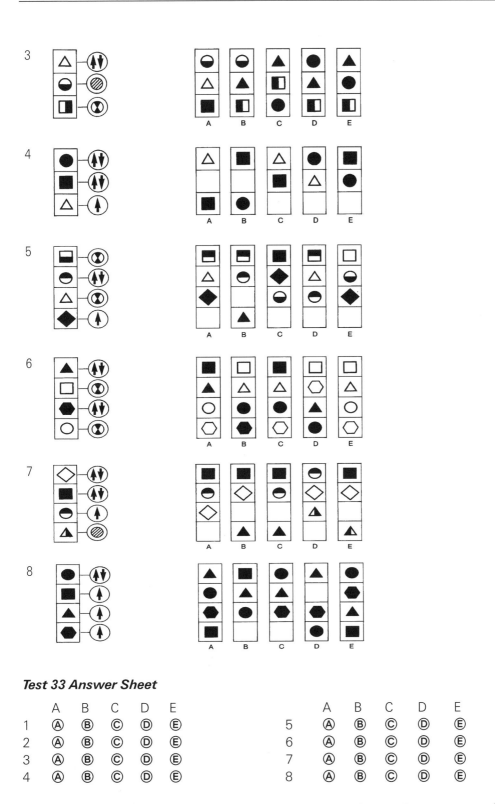

Test 33 Answer Sheet

	A	B	C	D	E			A	B	C	D	E
1	Ⓐ	Ⓑ	Ⓒ	Ⓓ	Ⓔ		5	Ⓐ	Ⓑ	Ⓒ	Ⓓ	Ⓔ
2	Ⓐ	Ⓑ	Ⓒ	Ⓓ	Ⓔ		6	Ⓐ	Ⓑ	Ⓒ	Ⓓ	Ⓔ
3	Ⓐ	Ⓑ	Ⓒ	Ⓓ	Ⓔ		7	Ⓐ	Ⓑ	Ⓒ	Ⓓ	Ⓔ
4	Ⓐ	Ⓑ	Ⓒ	Ⓓ	Ⓔ		8	Ⓐ	Ⓑ	Ⓒ	Ⓓ	Ⓔ

Test 34 Diagrammatic Reasoning

This abstract reasoning test measures your ability to infer a set of rules from a flow-chart, and apply these rules to new situations, and is specifically designed for the selection, development and promotion of staff working in the IT industry. It is a high-level measure of symbolic reasoning ability and is specially relevant in jobs that require the capacity to work through complex problems in a systematic and analytical manner, for example, in systems analysis and programming design.

Instructions: In this test you are shown a number of diagrams in which figures (shapes) in BOXES are altered by rules shown as symbols in CIRCLES. The rules can alter each figure by changing its colour, its size, its shape or by turning it upside down.

Paths through each diagram are shown as black or white arrows. You must follow paths which include only one type of arrow.

Work out what each rule does and then answer the questions below each diagram by filling in completely the appropriate circle on the answer sheet.

Time guideline: See how many questions you can answer in 4 minutes.

Look at the example below:

DIAGRAM

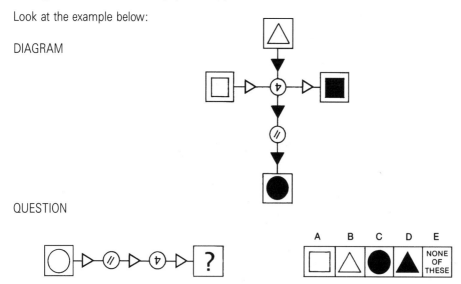

QUESTION

In the diagram, working horizontally, the white square becomes a black square so ↄ must be a colour changing rule. Working vertically, the white triangle becomes a black circle. Since we know that ↄ changes the colour of a figure, // must be a shape-changing rule. Applying these rules to the question, it is possible to identify that the white circle becomes a black triangle, so D is the correct answer to the question.

DIAGRAM

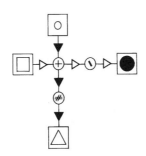

1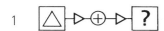

2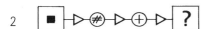

3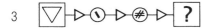

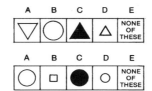

DIAGRAM

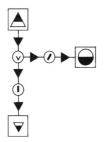

4

5

6

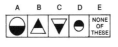

Test 34 Answer Sheet

	A	B	C	D	E
1	Ⓐ	Ⓑ	Ⓒ	Ⓓ	Ⓔ
2	Ⓐ	Ⓑ	Ⓒ	Ⓓ	Ⓔ
3	Ⓐ	Ⓑ	Ⓒ	Ⓓ	Ⓔ

	A	B	C	D	E
4	Ⓐ	Ⓑ	Ⓒ	Ⓓ	Ⓔ
5	Ⓐ	Ⓑ	Ⓒ	Ⓓ	Ⓔ
6	Ⓐ	Ⓑ	Ⓒ	Ⓓ	Ⓔ

Test 35 Diagrammatic Thinking

The following test measures your ability to apply checks and follow a sequence of symbols arranged in a logical order. This type of test is often used in the selection of qualified school leavers for modern apprenticeship schemes and other technically orientated jobs.

It is also used to select graduates applying to work in applied technical areas, for example, electronics technicians, electrical technicians, research technicians and also for jobs tracking process control systems, debugging software and systems design.

Instructions: In this test you are required to follow the progress of a 'Development figure' which is changed according to instructions contained in a series of 'Process boxes'. These boxes are divided into three levels, each of which affects the development figure in a given way.

Time guideline: There is no official time guideline for this practice test, however, try to work through the questions as quickly as you can. Remember that accuracy is equally as important as speed.

Process box		
Level 1	X	means change SHAPE from circle to square or vice versa
Level 2	X	means change SIZE from large to small or vice versa
Level 3	X	means change COLOUR from black to white or vice versa

NB: The absence of a cross means no change to that aspect of the figure.

Your task is to identify which process needs to be repeated at the end of the series in order to achieve the required 'Target' figure. Indicate your answer by fully blackening the appropriate circles A, B, C or D on Answer Sheet 35.

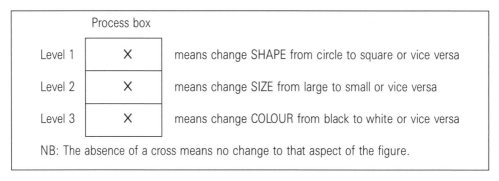

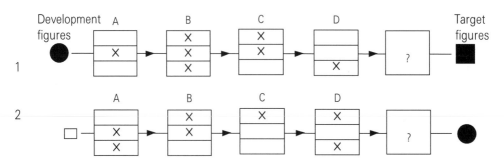

Test 35 Answer Sheet

	A	B	C	D
1	Ⓐ	Ⓑ	Ⓒ	Ⓓ
2	Ⓐ	Ⓑ	Ⓒ	Ⓓ

Answers to Abstract Reasoning questions

Test 31 Diagrammatic Series

	A	B	C	D	E
1	Ⓐ	Ⓑ	Ⓒ	Ⓓ	●
2	Ⓐ	●	Ⓒ	Ⓓ	Ⓔ
3	Ⓐ	Ⓑ	Ⓒ	●	Ⓔ
4	Ⓐ	Ⓑ	Ⓒ	●	Ⓔ
5	Ⓐ	Ⓑ	●	Ⓓ	Ⓔ
6	Ⓐ	●	Ⓒ	Ⓓ	Ⓔ
7	Ⓐ	●	Ⓒ	Ⓓ	Ⓔ
8	Ⓐ	Ⓑ	Ⓒ	Ⓓ	●

Test 32 Diagrammatic Reasoning

	A	B	C	D	E
1	Ⓐ	Ⓑ	Ⓒ	●	Ⓔ
2	Ⓐ	Ⓑ	Ⓒ	Ⓓ	●
3	Ⓐ	Ⓑ	●	Ⓓ	Ⓔ
4	Ⓐ	●	Ⓒ	Ⓓ	Ⓔ
5	●	Ⓑ	Ⓒ	Ⓓ	Ⓔ
6	Ⓐ	Ⓑ	Ⓒ	Ⓓ	●
7	Ⓐ	Ⓑ	Ⓒ	Ⓓ	●
8	Ⓐ	Ⓑ	Ⓒ	●	Ⓔ
9	Ⓐ	Ⓑ	●	Ⓓ	Ⓔ
10	●	Ⓑ	Ⓒ	Ⓓ	Ⓔ

Test 33 Diagramming

	A	B	C	D	E
1	Ⓐ	Ⓑ	Ⓒ	●	Ⓔ
2	Ⓐ	Ⓑ	●	Ⓓ	Ⓔ
3	Ⓐ	●	Ⓒ	Ⓓ	Ⓔ
4	Ⓐ	Ⓑ	Ⓒ	Ⓓ	●
5	●	Ⓑ	Ⓒ	Ⓓ	Ⓔ
6	Ⓐ	Ⓑ	Ⓒ	Ⓓ	●
7	Ⓐ	●	Ⓒ	Ⓓ	Ⓔ
8	Ⓐ	Ⓑ	●	Ⓓ	Ⓔ

Test 34 Diagrammatic Reasoning

	A	B	C	D	E
1	Ⓐ	●	Ⓒ	Ⓓ	Ⓔ
2	Ⓐ	Ⓑ	●	Ⓓ	Ⓔ
3	Ⓐ	Ⓑ	Ⓒ	●	Ⓔ
4	●	Ⓑ	Ⓒ	Ⓓ	Ⓔ
5	Ⓐ	Ⓑ	Ⓒ	●	Ⓔ
6	Ⓐ	Ⓑ	Ⓒ	Ⓓ	●

Test 35 Diagrammatic Thinking

	A	B	C	D
1	Ⓐ	Ⓑ	●	Ⓓ
2	●	Ⓑ	Ⓒ	Ⓓ

Abstract reasoning tests – how to improve your performance

- Try doing puzzles in newspapers, magazines and quiz books which involve diagrams.

- Play games which involve thinking out a problem visually and in a logical sequence, for example chess, Labyrinth, or computer Freecell.

- Abstract reasoning questions are often presented as sequences. Some are straightforward, but others require you to regard each shape, line, or symbol as a separate component working in its own independent way. For example, you might have a circle travelling in a clockwise direction, and a triangle going anticlockwise. Or one shape moving two spaces each time, another only one space.

- Watch out for shapes or lines which move in one direction, then another direction. Or shapes which alternate between hollow and filled in, or appear on the outside of an illustration and then on the inside etc.

- Don't be fazed by weird looking symbols or shapes, just study them until you see the pattern and how it changes from one illustration to the next. If you can work out what each separate element inside the illustration is doing as it progresses through the sequence, you can then predict how that component will appear in the next illustration in the series.

- People with dyslexia are often very good at abstract reasoning. They may have difficulty with words, but when it comes to logic, they're better than anyone else.

CHAPTER SIX

Spatial Reasoning

There are people who may not be so hot with words or numbers, but are good with space. They can see an object in their mind, and manipulate it, turn it round, upside down, or pull it in and out of shape. These people are said to have good spatial awareness, and they often find success in the field of design, illustration, architecture, publishing, technology, electronic engineering and IT. Therefore it is hardly surprising to find employers in these industries using spatial reasoning tests to select applicants for jobs which require three-dimensional perception.

The interesting thing about these test questions is that people with extremely good spatial awareness 'see' the solution immediately, without having to even think about it. People who are dyslexic often find this section easy as well. But for most of us, the answers are not so obvious and you might need to make more of an effort to manipulate the shapes in your mind (or even do as I do – physically turn the page round).

In common with other psychometric tests, spatial reasoning tests are strictly timed, and *every single question has one, and only one correct answer*.

In this chapter

In this chapter there are four different spatial reasoning psychometric tests for you to try. Before each one I've indicated for what sort of job, or industry, you might be expected to take that particular type of test.

At the end of this chapter there is section entitled **Spatial Reasoning Tests – How To Improve Your Performance** which is intended to help you do just that. Included in this section are some hints on tackling the questions themselves. If you have a problem with any of the questions then hopefully the advice contained in this section will get you back on track. Remember, however, that all of us have strengths and weaknesses, and everyone will have some difficulty with some of the tests in this book.

Test 36 Spatial Recognition

The following test measures your ability to recognise shapes in two dimensions. This type of test is often used in the selection and development of personnel in technically or practically orientated jobs. This test is also used to assess graduates because of its technical content.

Instructions: In this test you are to choose the shape on the right which is identical to the given shape. The identical shape may be rotated on the page but not turned over. Indicate your answers by filling in completely the appropriate circles on the answer sheet.

Time guideline: See how many questions you can answer in 2 minutes. Remember to work accurately as well as quickly.

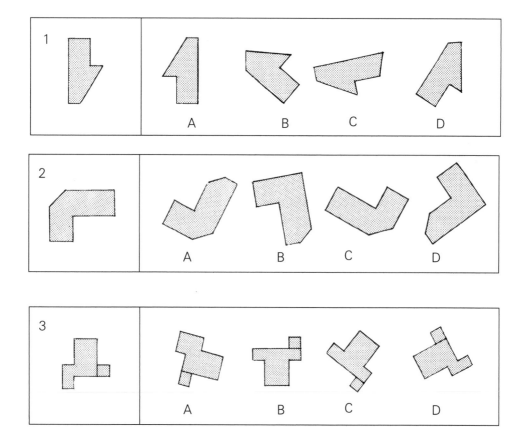

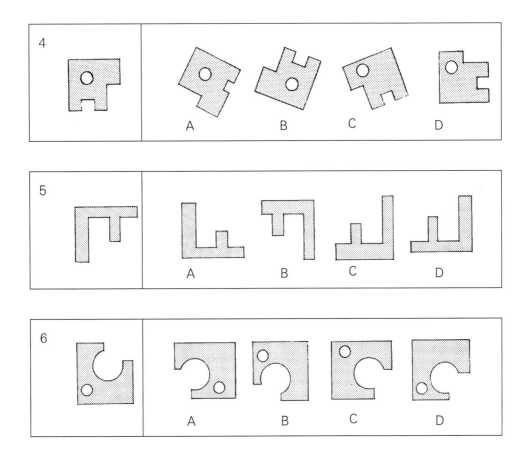

Test 36 Answer Sheet

	A	B	C	D
1	Ⓐ	Ⓑ	Ⓒ	Ⓓ
2	Ⓐ	Ⓑ	Ⓒ	Ⓓ
3	Ⓐ	Ⓑ	Ⓒ	Ⓓ
4	Ⓐ	Ⓑ	Ⓒ	Ⓓ
5	Ⓐ	Ⓑ	Ⓒ	Ⓓ
6	Ⓐ	Ⓑ	Ⓒ	Ⓓ

Test 37 Visual Estimation

The following test measures spatial perception and the ability to make accurate visual comparisons. This type of test is often used in the selection and development of personnel in technically or practically orientated jobs.

Instructions: In this test you are to choose the two shapes which are identical and fill in the appropriate *two* circles on the answer sheet.

Time guideline: See how many questions you can answer in 2 minutes. Remember to work accurately as well as quickly.

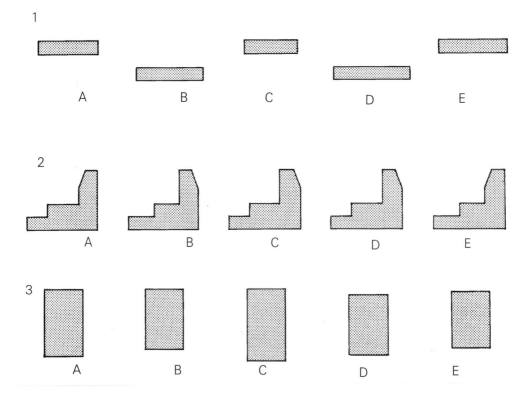

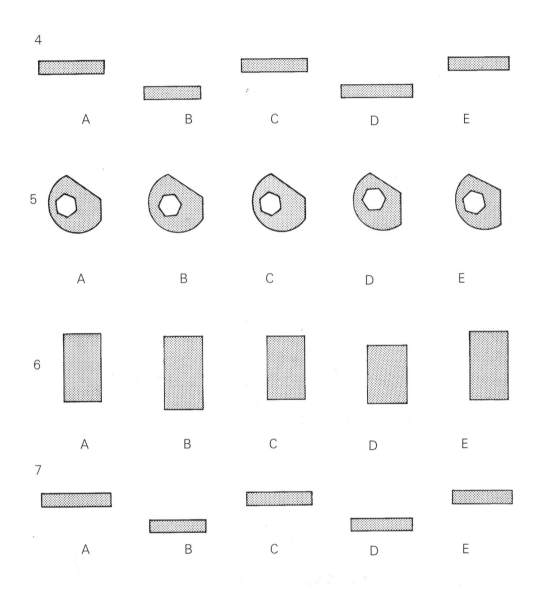

4

    A   B   C   D   E

5

    A   B   C   D   E

6

    A   B   C   D   E

7

    A   B   C   D   E

Test 37 Answer Sheet

	A	B	C	D	E
1	Ⓐ	Ⓑ	Ⓒ	Ⓓ	Ⓔ
2	Ⓐ	Ⓑ	Ⓒ	Ⓓ	Ⓔ
3	Ⓐ	Ⓑ	Ⓒ	Ⓓ	Ⓔ
4	Ⓐ	Ⓑ	Ⓒ	Ⓓ	Ⓔ
5	Ⓐ	Ⓑ	Ⓒ	Ⓓ	Ⓔ
6	Ⓐ	Ⓑ	Ⓒ	Ⓓ	Ⓔ
7	Ⓐ	Ⓑ	Ⓒ	Ⓓ	Ⓔ

Test 38 Spatial Reasoning

The following test measures your ability to visualise and manipulate shapes in three dimensions given a two-dimensional drawing. The test is high level, and could be used to select engineers, designers, draughtspeople and IT staff working with graphics or CAD/CAM software.

Instructions: In this test you are given a pattern which, if cut out, could be folded to make a three-dimensional shape (a box). You must decide which, if any, of the four boxes could be made by folding the pattern, and indicate this by filling in completely the appropriate circle on the answer sheet. If you think that none of the boxes could be made from the pattern, fill in circle 'E' on the answer sheet.

Time guideline: See how many questions you can answer in 3 minutes. Remember to work accurately as well as quickly.

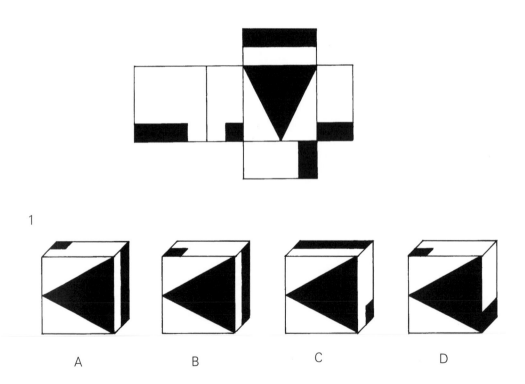

1

A	B	C	D

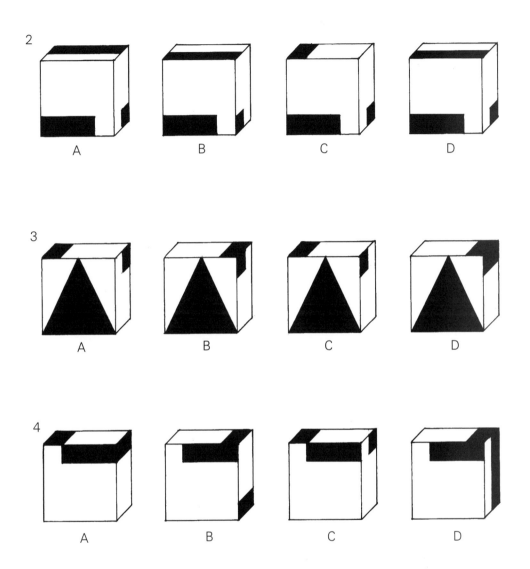

Test 38 Answer Sheet

	A	B	C	D	E
1	Ⓐ	Ⓑ	Ⓒ	Ⓓ	Ⓔ
2	Ⓐ	Ⓑ	Ⓒ	Ⓓ	Ⓔ
3	Ⓐ	Ⓑ	Ⓒ	Ⓓ	Ⓔ
4	Ⓐ	Ⓑ	Ⓒ	Ⓓ	Ⓔ

Test 39 Spatial Checking

This is another high level test, in this case measuring your ability to check designs and patterns. This type of test is used to select graduates in applied technology areas, for example, the design of electronic systems, engineering components and some applications of computer-aided design.

Instructions: In this test you are given a master layout with its own grid co-ordinates. To the right of this master layout are two copies, each of which differs from the master in one respect. Your task is to identify this difference and, using the co-ordinates shown on the master, indicate the grid reference by fully blackening the appropriate pair of circles on Answer Sheet 39. Note that copies are either rotated or flipped on the page.

Time guideline: There is no official time guideline, just work as quickly and accurately as you can.

MASTER

Test 39 Answer Sheet

1   ①   ②   ③   ④
    Ⓐ   Ⓑ   Ⓒ   Ⓓ

2   ①   ②   ③   ④
    Ⓐ   Ⓑ   Ⓒ   Ⓓ

Answers to Spatial Reasoning questions

Test 36 Spatial Recognition

	A	B	C	D
1	●	Ⓑ	Ⓒ	Ⓓ
2	Ⓐ	Ⓑ	●	Ⓓ
3	Ⓐ	Ⓑ	Ⓒ	●
4	Ⓐ	●	Ⓒ	Ⓓ
5	Ⓐ	Ⓑ	Ⓒ	●
6	Ⓐ	Ⓑ	●	Ⓓ

Test 37 Visual Estimation

	A	B	C	D	E
1	Ⓐ	●	Ⓒ	Ⓓ	●
2	Ⓐ	Ⓑ	●	●	Ⓔ
3	Ⓐ	●	Ⓒ	●	Ⓔ
4	●	Ⓑ	●	Ⓓ	Ⓔ
5	●	Ⓑ	●	Ⓓ	Ⓔ
6	●	Ⓑ	Ⓒ	Ⓓ	●
7	Ⓐ	Ⓑ	Ⓒ	●	●

Test 38 Spatial Reasoning

	A	B	C	D	E
1	Ⓐ	●	Ⓒ	Ⓓ	Ⓔ
2	Ⓐ	Ⓑ	Ⓒ	●	Ⓔ
3	Ⓐ	Ⓑ	●	Ⓓ	Ⓔ
4	Ⓐ	Ⓑ	Ⓒ	Ⓓ	●

Test 39 Spatial Checking

1	①	②	③	●
	Ⓐ	Ⓑ	●	Ⓓ

2	①	●	③	④
	Ⓐ	●	Ⓒ	Ⓓ

Spatial reasoning tests – how to improve your performance

◆ Look at plans and DIY manuals.

◆ Do jigsaw puzzles and play chess.

◆ Assemble construction sets.

◆ Make up plans, patterns and designs.

◆ Make up simple patterns and try to visualise what they would look like when rotated or flipped over.

◆ Imagine how various objects appear from different angles.

◆ Try drawing out the shapes in these tests on a sheet of paper. Actually handling the shapes and physically turning them round (or turning the book round) can help you understand how the 'puzzles' work.

◆ Try to get as much practice as you can.

◆ People with dyslexia are often very good at spatial reasoning. They may have difficulty with words, but 'see' the solutions to these puzzles immediately. Conversely, people who are very good at verbal reasoning may have trouble with this section – but we can't all be good at everything.

If all else fails, look at the test questions and answers at the same time. This should help you understand how these spatial reasoning problems work.

CHAPTER SEVEN

Mechanical Comprehension

Mechanical comprehension tests are written, multiple-choice psychometric tests which are used as part of the selection procedure for technically or practically orientated jobs. They test your understanding of how mechanical and technical things work.

To a certain extent, you either have this ability or you don't. If you can answer the test questions in this chapter easily, you're probably a very practical person and always have been. If, on the other hand, you're like me and are incapable of even programming the DVD without messing it up, it's unlikely that you'll be applying for a job in engineering or mechanics anyway.

But for those of you who are quite capable of taking your car to bits and putting the pieces back in the right places, I have included several rather easy mechanical comprehension tests for you to enjoy.

As with other psychometric tests, mechanical comprehension tests are strictly timed, and *every single question will have one, and only one correct answer.*

In this chapter

In this chapter there are 2 mechanical comprehension tests. Before each test I have indicated for what sort of job, or what industry, you might be expected to take that particular type of test.

At the end of this chapter there is section entitled **Mechanical Comprehension Tests – How To Improve Your Performance** which is intended to help you do just that. Included in this section are some hints on tackling the questions themselves. If you have a problem with any of the questions then hopefully the advice contained in this section will get you back on track. Remember, however, that all of us have strengths and weaknesses, and everyone will have some difficulty with some of the tests in this book.

Test 40 Mechanical Comprehension

This test assesses your understanding of basic mechanical principles and their application to such devices as pulleys and gears and simple structures.

This type of test is often used in the selection and development of individuals in technically or practically orientated jobs, and in engineering and mechanics.

Instructions: Each problem in the test consists of a question which refers to a drawing. Choose the best answer to each question, indicating your answer by filling in completely the appropriate circle on the answer sheet.

Time guideline: There are 4 questions – see how many you can do in 2 minutes.

1   With which spanner will it be easier to undo the nut?

If equal, mark C.

 A B

2   Which shelf will support the heaviest load?

3   In which direction can pulley-wheel 'X' turn?

If it cannot turn, mark C.

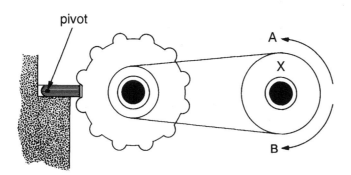

4   Which way will the pointer move when the shaft turns in the direction of the arrow?

If neither, mark C.

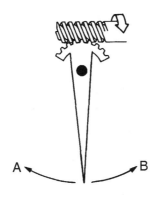

Test 40 Answer Sheet

	A	B	C
1	Ⓐ	Ⓑ	Ⓒ
2	Ⓐ	Ⓑ	Ⓒ
3	Ⓐ	Ⓑ	Ⓒ
4	Ⓐ	Ⓑ	Ⓒ

Test 41 Mechanical Comprehension

This test assesses your understanding of basic mechanical principles and their application to such devices as pulleys and gears and simple structures.

This type of test is often used in the selection and development of individuals in technically or practically orientated jobs. It is also used to recruit graduates or work experienced personnel moving into applied technology areas and jobs such as process control operators and electrical or research technicians, and in engineering and mechanics.

Instructions: The test is based on mechanical principles. Each problem in the test consists of a question which refers to a drawing. Choose the best answer to each question, indicating your answer by filling in completely the appropriate circle on the answer sheet.

Time guideline: There is no official time guideline for this practice test, however try to work through the questions as quickly as you can.

1 Which screw is more likely to pull out of the wall when a load is applied to the hook?

If equally likely, mark C.

2 Which apparatus requires less force to begin moving the block?

If equal, mark C.

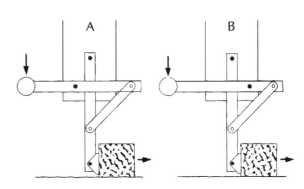

Test 41 Answer Sheet

	A	B	C
1	Ⓐ	Ⓑ	Ⓒ
2	Ⓐ	Ⓑ	Ⓒ

Answers to Mechanical Comprehension questions

Test 40 Mechanical Comprehension

	A	B	C
1	●	Ⓑ	Ⓒ
2	Ⓐ	Ⓑ	●
3	Ⓐ	●	Ⓒ
4	Ⓐ	●	Ⓒ

Test 41 Mechanical Comprehension

	A	B	C
1	●	Ⓑ	Ⓒ
2	Ⓐ	●	Ⓒ

Mechanical comprehension tests – how to improve your performance

- Attempt lots of DIY.

- Repair mechanical things when they break down, for example, the vacuum cleaner, a door lock.

- Take things to pieces and then reassemble them (assuming you're confident you actually can!).

- Try to understand how household objects work.

- Play with technical or construction sets.

- Build working models.

- Looking at the answers to the questions should give you a better understanding of the underlying mechanical principles involved.

- There are also plenty of books and websites on the subject but if you really can't manage this section, don't worry. Either you can do them, or you can't!

CHAPTER EIGHT

Fault Diagnosis

Fault diagnosis tests are written, multiple-choice psychometric tests which are used as part of the selection procedure for technically or practically orientated jobs, especially within the IT industry (often together with abstract reasoning tests). They assess your ability to identify faults in logical systems – an important skill which has many applications including those of electronics fault finding, debugging of software, process control systems and systems design.

Skill in this area is all about the application of logical deduction, coupled with common sense, patience and curiosity. A list of programming languages, technologies and operating environments which can develop your skills in this area is given at the end of the chapter.

As with other psychometric tests, fault diagnosis tests are strictly timed, and *every single question will have one, and only one correct answer.*

In this chapter

In this chapter there are two fault diagnosis practice tests for you to try. Before each test I have indicated for what sort of job, or for what industry, you might be expected to take that particular type of test.

At the end of this chapter there is section entitled **Fault Diagnosis Tests – How To Improve Your Performance** which is intended to help you do just that. However, remember that all of us have strengths and weaknesses, and everyone will have some difficulty with some of the tests in this book.

Test 42 Fault diagnosis

This test measures your ability to identify faults in systems. This type of test is often used in the selection of individuals in technically or practically orientated jobs such as skilled operatives, technical supervisors and jobs involving electronics fault finding. It is also used to test graduates because of its technical content.

Instructions: You are required to follow sequences made up of a number of switches labelled A, B, C, and D. Each switch, when working properly, has a specified effect on a set of numbered lights (shown in a rectangle on the left). The rectangle on the right contains the result of that sequence.

In each case, **one** of the switches is not working and has no effect on the numbered lights. A list of the switches and what they can do is shown below.

Time guideline: See how many questions you can answer in 3 minutes.

Switch	Effect when working
A	Turns 1 and 2 on/off i.e., black to white and vice versa
B	Turns 3 and 4 on/off i.e., black to white and vice versa
C	Turns 1 and 3 on/off i.e., black to white and vice versa
D	Turns 2 and 4 on/off i.e., black to white and vice versa

○ = ON
● = OFF
Remember – a switch not working has no effect

Your task is to identify the switch which is not working in each sequence and indicate this by fully blackening the appropriate circle on Answer Sheet 42.

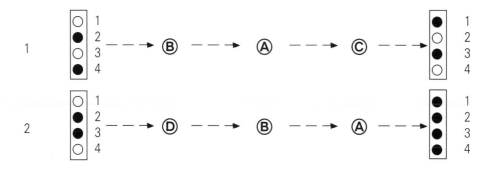

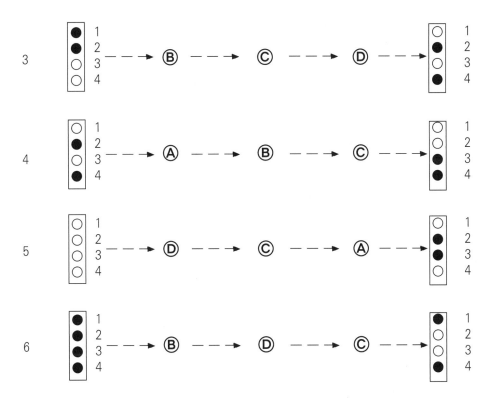

Test 42 Answer Sheet

	A	B	C	D
1	Ⓐ	Ⓑ	Ⓒ	Ⓓ
2	Ⓐ	Ⓑ	Ⓒ	Ⓓ
3	Ⓐ	Ⓑ	Ⓒ	Ⓓ
4	Ⓐ	Ⓑ	Ⓒ	Ⓓ
5	Ⓐ	Ⓑ	Ⓒ	Ⓓ
6	Ⓐ	Ⓑ	Ⓒ	Ⓓ

Test 43 Fault finding

This test measures your ability to identify faults in systems. This type of test is often used in the selection of graduates or work-experienced personnel moving into applied technology areas. Uses include electronics fault finding, debugging of software, process control systems and systems design.

Instructions: You are required to follow sequences made up of a number of switches labelled A, B and C. Each switch, when working properly, has a specified effect on a set of numbered lights (shown in a square on the left). The circle on the right contains the result of a particular sequence.

In each case, **one** of the switches is not working and so has no effect on the numbered lights. A list of the switches and what they can do is shown below.

Time guideline: There is no official time guideline for this test. However, try to work through the questions as quickly and as accurately as possible.

Switch	Effect when working
A	Turns 1 and 3 on/off i.e. from black to white or vice versa
B	Turns 3 and 4 on/off i.e. from black to white or vice versa
C	Turns 2 and 4 on/off i.e. from black to white or vice versa
	Remember – a switch that is not working has no effect

Your task is to identify the switch which is not working and indicate this by fully blackening the appopriate circles A, B or C on Answer Sheet 43.

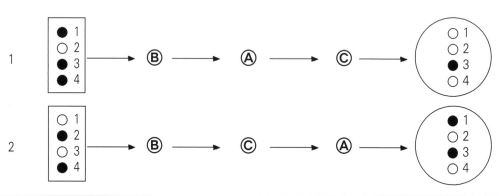

Test 43 Answer Sheet

	A	B	C
1	Ⓐ	Ⓑ	Ⓒ
2	Ⓐ	Ⓑ	Ⓒ

Answers to Fault Diagnosis questions

Test 42 Fault Diagnosis

	A	B	C	D
1	Ⓐ	Ⓑ	●	Ⓓ
2	Ⓐ	●	Ⓒ	Ⓓ
3	Ⓐ	Ⓑ	Ⓒ	●
4	Ⓐ	●	Ⓒ	Ⓓ
5	Ⓐ	Ⓑ	Ⓒ	●
6	Ⓐ	Ⓑ	●	Ⓓ

Test 43 Fault Finding

	A	B	C
1	Ⓐ	Ⓑ	●
2	Ⓐ	●	Ⓒ

Fault diagnosis tests – how to improve your performance

For the IT industry you need to have the key tools of the trade – programming languages, technologies and operating environments, so perhaps learn some of the following:

- Programming languages such as HTML, XML/XSL, Basic, Visual Basic, C++, Java, .NET (including : ASP.NET, C# (pronounced 'Cee sharp'), VB.NET) and use them as much as possible.
- Relational database skills such as SQL, T-SQL.

Here's an additional list of languages and technologies to consider:

- Scripting: Javascript, VBScript, Perl
- Web: HTTP, HTML, XML, XSL, ASP, JSP, Servlets, J2EE, .NET
- Interactive web and CD-ROM: Macromedia Flash and Director
- Web services: WSDL, SOAP
- Componentware: DCOM, COM+, EJB
- Databases: SQL Server, Oracle, DB2, Sybase
- EAI: Oracle, SAP, Ariba, Agresso, CedAr
- Mail systems: Exchange, Domino, ESMTP, X.400
- Directory systems: LDAP, X.500, Active Directory
- Security infrastructure: PKI, SSL, Kerberos, PGP
- Windows platforms: 95, 98, NT, 2000, XP
- Unix platforms: Solaris, Linux, AIX, HP-UX, Mac OS X

Additionally you could:

- Take an electronics course.
- Think about the things that can go wrong with a piece of equipment, for example, a car, a washing machine etc. What effect would any particular fault have? How would you diagnose the fault? What tests would pinpoint where the fault lay?

For all these ideas there's simply no substitute for hands-on practical experience. At the beginning of this chapter I said that skill in this area is all about the application of logical deduction coupled with common sense, patience and curiosity. If you already possess those qualities, **practical experience** – i.e. using the programmes or languages as much as possible – is the thing which will most improve your performance in this area.

CHAPTER NINE

Accuracy Tests

Tests that measure accuracy have various names. They can be called 'acuity' tests, or 'clerical tests', but whatever the label they all basically do the same thing. They are multiple choice tests which measure your ability to:

✓ deal with information

✓ follow rules and instructions precisely

✓ work at high speed

✓ check material for errors

✓ maintain a high level of accuracy and concentration.

If you are applying for a job involving administrative or clerical work, recording or checking of data or anything else requiring close attention to detail, you may have to take one or more accuracy test. The tests can range from basic right up to graduate level.

Accuracy tests are strictly timed, and *every single question will have one, and only one correct answer.*

In this chapter

In this chapter there are 11 different tests for you to try. Before each one I've indicated for what sort of job, or what industry, you might be expected to take that particular type of test. Even if you think some of the tests are fairly basic, have a go. They are a good way to train your brain to concentrate – very useful if you're impatient or not used to paying attention to fine detail.

At the end of this chapter there is section entitled **Accuracy Tests – How To Improve Your Performance** which is intended to help you do just that. Included in this section are some hints on tackling the questions themselves. If you have a problem with any of the questions then hopefully the advice contained in this section will get you back on track. However, remember that all of us have strengths and weaknesses, and everyone will have some difficulty with some of the tests in this book.

Test 44 Understanding Instructions

This test measures understanding of written information at a fairly basic level. It's designed for people applying for technical and transport jobs. If you find it very easy, use it as a warm up for the tests that follow later in this chapter.

Instructions: In this test you are given a written passage containing instructions. Use the instructions in the passage to answer the questions which follow. Choose the right answer from the four answers given and blacken the correct circle A, B, C or D on your answer sheet.

Time guideline: There is no time limit for this test, however try to work as quickly and accurately as you can.

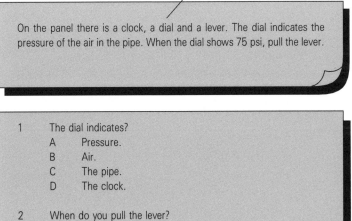

On the panel there is a clock, a dial and a lever. The dial indicates the pressure of the air in the pipe. When the dial shows 75 psi, pull the lever.

1   The dial indicates?
    A   Pressure.
    B   Air.
    C   The pipe.
    D   The clock.

2   When do you pull the lever?
    A   When there is air in the pipe.
    B   When the dial shows 75 psi.
    C   When there is a clock.
    D   When there is a clock, dial and a lever.

3   What is on the panel?
    A   A clock only.
    B   A clock and a lever only.
    C   A clock and a lever and a dial.
    D   A clock and a lever and a dial and air.

Test 44 Answer Sheet

	A	B	C	D
1	Ⓐ	Ⓑ	Ⓒ	Ⓓ
2	Ⓐ	Ⓑ	Ⓒ	Ⓓ
3	Ⓐ	Ⓑ	Ⓒ	Ⓓ

Test 45 Basic Checking

This test measure speed and accuracy of checking at a basic level. This type of test is often used to select clerical staff whose job includes routine checking.

Instructions: Find the two codes which are the same in each line and mark the letters for the two appropriate columns in the answer section by filling in completely the appropriate circles on the answer sheet.

Time guideline: There are 14 questions – see how many you can do in 2 minutes.

	A	B	C	D	E
1	6522	5262	6252	6522	6225
2	SSGB	SGSB	SSBG	GBSS	SSBG
3	8553	8535	5852	8535	8355
4	YWHN	YHWN	YWHN	YNWH	NYWH
5	57657	57675	57675	56675	57765
6	ZHHCZ	ZZCHH	ZCHHZ	ZCZHH	ZCHHZ
7	82443	84243	84234	84342	84243
8	LBENI	LEBNI	LIBNE	LBNEI	LBNEI
9	232215	232125	231225	232125	232151
10	JWHRWF	JWHWRF	JWHRWF	JFWHRW	JHWWRF
11	9760207	9760270	9706207	9760027	9760207

12	MUBFBII	MUBFIBI	MUBBFII	MBBUFII	MUBBFII
13	56932099	56923099	56930299	56932099	56392099
14	YBZGOCXF	YBZOGXCF	YBZOGCXF	YBZOGCXF	YZBOGCXF

Test 45 Answer Sheet

	A	B	C	D	E
1	Ⓐ	Ⓑ	Ⓒ	Ⓓ	Ⓔ
2	Ⓐ	Ⓑ	Ⓒ	Ⓓ	Ⓔ
3	Ⓐ	Ⓑ	Ⓒ	Ⓓ	Ⓔ
4	Ⓐ	Ⓑ	Ⓒ	Ⓓ	Ⓔ
5	Ⓐ	Ⓑ	Ⓒ	Ⓓ	Ⓔ
6	Ⓐ	Ⓑ	Ⓒ	Ⓓ	Ⓔ
7	Ⓐ	Ⓑ	Ⓒ	Ⓓ	Ⓔ
8	Ⓐ	Ⓑ	Ⓒ	Ⓓ	Ⓔ
9	Ⓐ	Ⓑ	Ⓒ	Ⓓ	Ⓔ
10	Ⓐ	Ⓑ	Ⓒ	Ⓓ	Ⓔ
11	Ⓐ	Ⓑ	Ⓒ	Ⓓ	Ⓔ
12	Ⓐ	Ⓑ	Ⓒ	Ⓓ	Ⓔ
13	Ⓐ	Ⓑ	Ⓒ	Ⓓ	Ⓔ
14	Ⓐ	Ⓑ	Ⓒ	Ⓓ	Ⓔ

Test 46 Clerical Checking

This test measures speed and accuracy in checking detailed information. This type of test is often used to select clerical and administrative staff of all types.

Instructions: You are required to check that the hand-written information about sports centre bookings has been typed accurately. You should note any errors according to the following rules:

Fill in circle:

A = errors in name
B = errors in time
C = errors in date
D = errors in facilities
E = no errors

Indicate your answers by filling in completely the appropriate circles in the answer section.

Time guideline: There are 15 questions – see how many you can do in 3 minutes.

	Name	Time	Date	Tennis	Badminton	Gymnasium	Solarium
1	BROOK	8 am	13.8	✓			
2	DRUMMOND	7 am	24.8			✓	✓
3	CRIAG	9 am	26.9		✓		
4	JONES	7.30 am	15.9	✓		✓	
5	PATEL	3.25 pm	7.11			✓	
6	BROWN	6.15 pm	19.9				✓
7	HILL	7.10 pm	17.8		✓		
8	PHILIPS	2.30 pm	6.11	✓			✓
9	ADAMS	9.40 am	17.9			✓	
10	SINGH	4.50 pm	13.9		✓		
11	CHAN	11.25 pm	9.10	✓			
12	YOUNG	10.30 am	29.10			✓	✓
13	WILLIAMS	12.15 am	18.11			✓	
14	SAMUELS	11.25 am	26.10		✓		
15	MAN	10.30 am	30.10	✓			✓

	Name	Time	Date	Facilities			
1	Brook	8am	23.8	🎾			
2	Drummond	7pm	24.8			🏋	
3	Craig	9am	26.9		🏸		
4	Jones	7.30am	15.9	🎾		🏋	
5	Patel	3.25pm	7.10		🏸		
6	Brown	6.15pm	19.9	🎾			
7	Hall	7.10am	25.9			🏋	
8	Philips	2.30am	6.11	🎾			☀
9	Adams	9.40am	17.9			🏋	
10	Singh	4.50pm	13.9		🏸		☀
11	Chan	1.25pm	9.10	🎾			
12	Young	10.30am	29.10			🏋	☀
13	Williams	12.15pm	18.11			🏋	
14	Samuels	11.25am	26.10	🎾			
15	Mann	10.40am	30.11	🎾			☀

SYMBOLS

TENNIS 🎾
BADMINTON 🏸
GYMNASIUM 🏋
SOLARIUM ☀

Test 46 Answer Sheet

	A	B	C	D	E
1	Ⓐ	Ⓑ	Ⓒ	Ⓓ	Ⓔ
2	Ⓐ	Ⓑ	Ⓒ	Ⓓ	Ⓔ
3	Ⓐ	Ⓑ	Ⓒ	Ⓓ	Ⓔ
4	Ⓐ	Ⓑ	Ⓒ	Ⓓ	Ⓔ
5	Ⓐ	Ⓑ	Ⓒ	Ⓓ	Ⓔ
6	Ⓐ	Ⓑ	Ⓒ	Ⓓ	Ⓔ
7	Ⓐ	Ⓑ	Ⓒ	Ⓓ	Ⓔ
8	Ⓐ	Ⓑ	Ⓒ	Ⓓ	Ⓔ
9	Ⓐ	Ⓑ	Ⓒ	Ⓓ	Ⓔ
10	Ⓐ	Ⓑ	Ⓒ	Ⓓ	Ⓔ
11	Ⓐ	Ⓑ	Ⓒ	Ⓓ	Ⓔ
12	Ⓐ	Ⓑ	Ⓒ	Ⓓ	Ⓔ
13	Ⓐ	Ⓑ	Ⓒ	Ⓓ	Ⓔ
14	Ⓐ	Ⓑ	Ⓒ	Ⓓ	Ⓔ
15	Ⓐ	Ⓑ	Ⓒ	Ⓓ	Ⓔ

Test 47 Checking Information

This test also measures understanding of written information at a fairly basic level. It's designed for people applying for jobs in admin and transport. If you find it very easy, use it as a warm up for the tests that follow later in this chapter.

Instructions: In this section you are presented with tables showing the names of 15 stations divided into 5 zones, V to Z. For each question you have to decide which of the five tickets shown would be the correct one to issue. When you have made your selection, mark the appropriate circle A, B, C or D on your answer sheet by filling in completely the appropriate circle on the answer sheet.

Both the departure and destination zones should be included when counting the number of zones covered by any particular journey. For example, a journey from X to Z would count as three zones; W to X would be two zones.

Now try the questions using the information below.

Time guideline: There is no time limit for this test, however try to work as quickly and accurately as you can.

V	W	X	Y	Z
Fitch	Montown	Denner	Benton	Carlow
Newhall	Parks	Hershey	Ridley	Embridge
Shothill	Woodlow	Addon	Jarrat	Gallant

Journey	Fare
Within 1 zone	10 pence
Across 2 zones	20 pence
Across 3 zones	30 pence
Across 4 zones	40 pence
Across 5 zones	50 pence

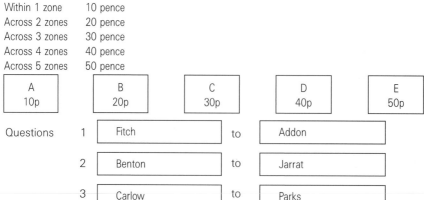

A	B	C	D	E
10p	20p	30p	40p	50p

Questions	1	Fitch	to	Addon
	2	Benton	to	Jarrat
	3	Carlow	to	Parks

Test 47 Answer Sheet

	A	B	C	D	E
1	Ⓐ	Ⓑ	Ⓒ	Ⓓ	Ⓔ
2	Ⓐ	Ⓑ	Ⓒ	Ⓓ	Ⓔ
3	Ⓐ	Ⓑ	Ⓒ	Ⓓ	Ⓔ

Test 48 Visual Checking

This test also measures understanding of written information and ability to follow simple instructions in a slightly more technical context. It's designed for people applying for jobs in production, modern apprenticeship schemes and other technically orientated jobs.

Instructions: In this test you have to find the correct row of switches that goes with a set of lights. The rules that link the lights and switches are shown below. Fill in completely the appropriate circle on the answer sheet.

Time guideline: There is no time limit for this test, however try to work as quickly and accurately as you can.

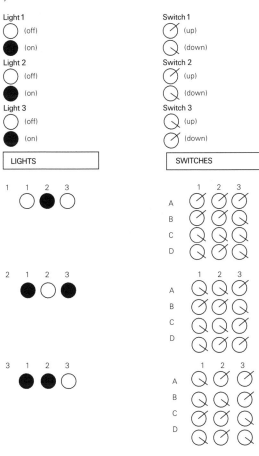

Test 48 Answer Sheet

	A	B	C	D
1	Ⓐ	Ⓑ	Ⓒ	Ⓓ
2	Ⓐ	Ⓑ	Ⓒ	Ⓓ
3	Ⓐ	Ⓑ	Ⓒ	Ⓓ

Test 49 Computer Checking

This test measures your ability to check input information with the corresponding output, i.e., the accurate recording of new data onto a VDU screen or computer printout. The information may be reordered in some way, requiring both checking and scanning ability, as well as an element of simple reasoning.

This type of test is often used to select school leavers and work-experienced applicants, both at the clerical and supervisory level, in a variety of organisations including building societies, banks, retailers and many public sector organisations. Examples of jobs include accounts clerks, clerical supervisors, mail order clerks and all office staff using VDUs.

Instructions: You are required to identify quickly and accurately whether the information has been correctly transferred to a VDU screen or computer printout. The output may be re-ordered in some way.

If there is an error in line 1 of the original document, fill in completely box A. If there is an error in line 2 of the original document, fill in completely box B. If there is an error in line 3 of the original document, fill in completely box C. If there is an error in line 4 of the original document, fill in completely box D. If there are no errors, fill in completely box E.

Time guideline: There is no official time guideline for this test. However, try to work through the questions as quickly and as accurately as possible.

1
Customer	582		
Invoice	X398		
Quantity	2	Size	36
Item	PD877	Value	18.99

2
Customer	379		
Invoice	X757		
Quantity	2	Size	10
Item	DX786	Value	9.50

3
Customer	323		
Invoice	Z819		
Quantity	3	Size	18
Item	ZX334	Value	36.90

4
Customer	414		
Invoice	B564		
Quantity	4	Size	18
Item	BT311	Value	31.99

114825 – 3			GENERAL COMMUNICATION AD5461		
RUN 4112			DATE 17 AUGUST		
INVOICE	CUSTOMER	QUANTITY	ITEM	SIZE	VALUE
X398	582	1	PD877	36	18.99
X757	397	2	DX786	12	9.50
Y213	664	1	LT468	40	25.00
Z819	323	3	ZX334	18	36.90
A742	443	5	BX021	2	12.50
B546	414	4	BT311	4	11.99
C611	452	1	BR121	6	2.49
C774	538	2	DX222	10	14.50
D775	543	1	BT223	11	15.00
D413	622	3	PT314	8	17.99
D276	422	6	ZD224	3	42.60
E119	123	3	LZ123	40	74.99
E772	232	1	DX223	10	14.22
E231	197	1	DX223	14	14.22
F332	772	1	BX223	4	15.00
F644	185	2	TD124	8	14.00
			END RUN 5421358 – 4		

Test 49 Answer Sheet

	A	B	C	D	E
1	Ⓐ	Ⓑ	Ⓒ	Ⓓ	Ⓔ
2	Ⓐ	Ⓑ	Ⓒ	Ⓓ	Ⓔ
3	Ⓐ	Ⓑ	Ⓒ	Ⓓ	Ⓔ
4	Ⓐ	Ⓑ	Ⓒ	Ⓓ	Ⓔ

Test 50 Classification

This test measures understanding of written information and attention to detail. It's designed for people applying for admin and clerical jobs which have some element of filing, data processing, checking or recording.

Instructions: In this test, you are to classify library cards by giving them filing codes. There are two kinds of cards, those to be filed by author and those to be filed by subject. The way the card is to be filed is shown at the top of each one, where either author or subject has been typed. Fill in completely the appropriate circle on the answer sheet.

Author cards are given codes alphabetically, according to the last name of the author marked on the card.

Subject cards are given codes according to the subject mentioned on the card.

Time guideline: There is no time limit for this test, however try to work as quickly and accurately as you can.

AUTHOR INDEIX						SUBJECT INDEX					
	A	B	C	D	E		A	B	C	D	E
Aaron – Halwood	●	Ⓑ	Ⓒ	Ⓓ	Ⓔ	Arts & Crafts	Ⓐ	Ⓑ	Ⓒ	Ⓔ	●
Hambrow – Martin	Ⓐ	●	Ⓒ	Ⓓ	Ⓔ	Cookery	●	●	Ⓒ	Ⓓ	Ⓔ
Mead – Singh	Ⓐ	Ⓑ	●	Ⓓ	Ⓔ	Sports	●	Ⓑ	●	Ⓓ	Ⓔ
Sippett – Zuckerman	Ⓐ	Ⓑ	Ⓒ	●	Ⓔ	Travel & Maps	●	Ⓑ	Ⓒ	●	Ⓔ

See how many you can do in 3 minutes.

1	SHELTON LIBRARY

AUTHOR

Author: Jones, R

Title: Cooking for pleasure

2	SHELTON LIBRARY

SUBJECT

Author: Hail, L

Title: The Olympic Sports Handbook

3	SHELTON LIBRARY

SUBJECT

Author: Murray, J

Title: The World Atlas

4	SHELTON LIBRARY

SUBJECT

Author: Patel, C

Title: Portrait Painting

5	SHELTON LIBRARY

SUBJECT

Author: Townsend, A

Title: The Good Travelling Guide

6	SHELTON LIBRARY

AUTHOR

Author: Benn, E

Title: The Low Fat Diet Book

7	SHELTON LIBRARY

AUTHOR

Author: Jarvis, T

Title: The Craft of Carpentry

8	SHELTON LIBRARY

SUBJECT

Author: Jones, R

Title: Cooking for pleausre

9	SHELTON LIBRARY

SUBJECT

Author: Fielding, M

Title: Snooker or Pool?

10	SHELTON LIBRARY

SUBJECT

Author: Horne, V

Title: Vegetarian Gourmet

11	SHELTON LIBRARY

AUTHOR

Author: Sullivan, R

Title: French Cooking Step by Step

12	SHELTON LIBRARY

AUTHOR

Author: Dougherty, S

Title: The Beginners Guide to Needlework

Test 50 Answer Sheet

	A	B	C	D	E
1	Ⓐ	Ⓑ	Ⓒ	Ⓓ	Ⓔ
2	Ⓐ	Ⓑ	Ⓒ	Ⓓ	Ⓔ
3	Ⓐ	Ⓑ	Ⓒ	Ⓓ	Ⓔ
4	Ⓐ	Ⓑ	Ⓒ	Ⓓ	Ⓔ
5	Ⓐ	Ⓑ	Ⓒ	Ⓓ	Ⓔ
6	Ⓐ	Ⓑ	Ⓒ	Ⓓ	Ⓔ

	A	B	C	D	E
7	Ⓐ	Ⓑ	Ⓒ	Ⓓ	Ⓔ
8	Ⓐ	Ⓑ	Ⓒ	Ⓓ	Ⓔ
9	Ⓐ	Ⓑ	Ⓒ	Ⓓ	Ⓔ
10	Ⓐ	Ⓑ	Ⓒ	Ⓓ	Ⓔ
11	Ⓐ	Ⓑ	Ⓒ	Ⓓ	Ⓔ
12	Ⓐ	Ⓑ	Ⓒ	Ⓓ	Ⓔ

Test 51 Following Instructions

This test measures your ability to understand and follow written instructions. The topic covered is relevant to a technical environment although no prior knowledge of technical words is assumed.

  This type of test is often used to select staff for modern apprenticeship schemes and other technically orientated jobs. It is also used to select graduates applying to work in applied technical areas, for example, electronics technicians, electrical technicians and research technicians.

Instructions: In this test you are given a written passage containing instructions. Use the instructions in the passage to answer the questions which follow. Indicate your answers each time by filling in completely the appropriate circle A, B, C or D.

Time guideline: There is no official time guideline for this test. However, try to work through the questions as quickly and as accurately as possible.

Photocopier Operation

Push the SORTER switch if the sorter is to be used to collate the copies (i.e. separate them into sets). The sort indicator is lit when this switch is on. If the lamp flashes, check the position of the sorter.

NO SORT mode up to 99 copies can be made, all delivered to the top bin.

SORT mode 15 copies can be made from each original. The original can be up to 30 pages long. One copy of each original is delivered to each bin.

Originals should be arranged in reverse order when using the SORT mode.

---

1   What should you do if the sorter indicator flashes?

A Push the SORTER switch.

B Check the position of the sorter.

C Disconnect the sorter.

D Collate manually.

2   What is the maximum number of pages a document can have if the sorter is to be used?

A 15.

B 99.

C 30.

D No limit.

Test 51 Answer Sheet

	A	B	C	D
1	Ⓐ	Ⓑ	Ⓒ	Ⓓ
2	Ⓐ	Ⓑ	Ⓒ	Ⓓ

Test 52 Coded Instructions

This test measures your ability to understand and follow written instructions when used in the form of coded language.

This type of test is often used to select school leavers and work-experienced applicants, both at the clerical and supervisory level in a variety of organisations including building societies, banks, retailers and many public sector organisations. Examples of jobs include accounts clerks, clerical supervisors, mail order clerks and all office staff using VDUs.

Instructions: The test consists of a series of passages containing instructions, each of which is followed by a number of questions. You are required to use the instructions in each passage to answer the questions which follow that passage. Indicate your answers each time by filling in completely the appropriate box A, B, C, D or E.

Time guideline: There is no official time guideline for this test. However, try to work through the questions as quickly and as accurately as possible.

Records Check

You are carrying out a computer check of personnel records.

If the staff member has left the organisation enter code L alone into the computer. For all staff members still present enter code P together with the appropriate check code below.

If the home address has changed enter code A: otherwise enter code B. If the home telephone number has changed enter code T. If the home telephone number is the same enter code C.

If the name of the staff member's doctor has changed enter code D: otherwise enter code N. If the doctor's telephone number has changed enter code R: if the telephone number is the same enter code S.

Code letters are to be entered in the sequence given above.

Which codes should be used to show the following records?

1 Employee number 1 is still a staff member. His address has changed but he has kept the same telephone number. There is no change to his doctor's details.

   A   P A N S

   B   A C N S

   C   P A C N S

   D   P A N C S

   E   P A C S N

2 Employee number 2 changed her doctor a year ago but in the past month has left the organisation.

A   L R

B   L N R

C   R L

D   L

E   L R N

3 Employee number 3 is still a staff member. His address and telephone number are the same and so is the name of his doctor. However, his doctor is operating from a different address and telephone number.

A   P B C R

B   P B C R N

C   P C N

D   L P B C R

E   P B C N R

4 Employee number 4 is still a staff member. Her address and telephone number are unchanged. Her doctor's name and telephone number are unchanged.

A   P B N

B   P B C N S

C   P N S B C

D   P A C N S

E   P B T N S

Test 52 Answer Sheet

	A	B	C	D	E
1	Ⓐ	Ⓑ	Ⓒ	Ⓓ	Ⓔ
2	Ⓐ	Ⓑ	Ⓒ	Ⓓ	Ⓔ
3	Ⓐ	Ⓑ	Ⓒ	Ⓓ	Ⓔ
4	Ⓐ	Ⓑ	Ⓒ	Ⓓ	Ⓔ

Test 53 Computer Checking

This test measures speed and accuracy in the checking of character strings made up of letters, numbers and symbols. These are important skills in any area of programming and especially important for computer data entry staff. This type of test is designed for applicants with A level to graduate qualifications, or similar.

Instructions: Find the two sets of characters which are the same in each line and mark the letters for the two appropriate columns (A, B, C, D or E) on the answer section by filling in completely the appropriate circle on the answer sheet.

Time guideline: There are 20 questions – see how many you can do in 3 minutes.

	A	B	C	D	E
1	15*TZ	1*5TZ	15*T2	15*TZ	IS*TZ
2	TVB$	TBV$	TBVS	TB$V	TBV$
3	GS24B	G2S4B	GS24B	GS2B4	GS428
4	LOGGB	LO6GB	LOGG8	LOG68	LOG68
5	$*T(	$*T(	$*2(	S*2(	$*T)
6	986538	968538	986588	968538	998538
7	B27JP	B2J7P	B277P	B27PP	B277P
8	PC4#!	PC7#!	PC47!	PC4#1	PC4#!
9	GA!9%	GA!98	GA198	GA!98	GA19%
10	D*8XD	D*X*D	DX8XD	DX8XD	D*86D
11	969G)	669G)	696G)	669G)	669G)
12	EO((()	EO(()	EO(())	EO(())	EO()))
13	HEX09	HEX07	#EX09	H4X0P	HEX09
14	47S$	44S$$	47S$$	44SS$	44S$$
15	NVBR	NVR8	NVRB	NVRB	NVBB
16	69LBJ	69BLJ	99LBJ	69LBJ	69LJB
17	TXENE	TTENE	TXENN	TEXNE	TXENE

18	08%%Q	088%Q	0%8%Q	Q8%%Q	088%Q
19	LOP23	LOB23	LOP32	LOB32	LOB23
20	A79QA	A7Q9A	A790A	A970A	A970A

Test 53 Answer Sheet

	A	B	C	D	E
1	Ⓐ	Ⓑ	Ⓒ	Ⓓ	Ⓔ
2	Ⓐ	Ⓑ	Ⓒ	Ⓓ	Ⓔ
3	Ⓐ	Ⓑ	Ⓒ	Ⓓ	Ⓔ
4	Ⓐ	Ⓑ	Ⓒ	Ⓓ	Ⓔ
5	Ⓐ	Ⓑ	Ⓒ	Ⓓ	Ⓔ
6	Ⓐ	Ⓑ	Ⓒ	Ⓓ	Ⓔ
7	Ⓐ	Ⓑ	Ⓒ	Ⓓ	Ⓔ
8	Ⓐ	Ⓑ	Ⓒ	Ⓓ	Ⓔ
9	Ⓐ	Ⓑ	Ⓒ	Ⓓ	Ⓔ
10	Ⓐ	Ⓑ	Ⓒ	Ⓓ	Ⓔ
11	Ⓐ	Ⓑ	Ⓒ	Ⓓ	Ⓔ
12	Ⓐ	Ⓑ	Ⓒ	Ⓓ	Ⓔ
13	Ⓐ	Ⓑ	Ⓒ	Ⓓ	Ⓔ
14	Ⓐ	Ⓑ	Ⓒ	Ⓓ	Ⓔ
15	Ⓐ	Ⓑ	Ⓒ	Ⓓ	Ⓔ
16	Ⓐ	Ⓑ	Ⓒ	Ⓓ	Ⓔ
17	Ⓐ	Ⓑ	Ⓒ	Ⓓ	Ⓔ
18	Ⓐ	Ⓑ	Ⓒ	Ⓓ	Ⓔ
19	Ⓐ	Ⓑ	Ⓒ	Ⓓ	Ⓔ
20	Ⓐ	Ⓑ	Ⓒ	Ⓓ	Ⓔ

Test 54 Syntax Checking

This test measures your ability to check material quickly and accurately. These are important skills in any area of programming and especially important for computer data entry staff, software engineers, systems analysts, programmers and database administrators. This type of test is designed for applicants with graduate qualifications, or similar.

Instructions: In this test you will find lines taken from a mock programming language. Some lines do not conform to the rules of the language. Your task is to find which rules (if any) have been broken.

The rules for building these lines are found in the boxes below. There are two sorts of lines: those specified by an 'X' and those specified by a 'Y'. Each sort of line has its own set of 3 rules.

Using the appropriate set of rules, you must check which, if any, of the 3 rules have been broken. If a rule has been broken, fill in the appropriate circle on the answer sheet. More than one rule may be broken, so you may need to fill in more than one circle. If no rule has been broken, fill in circle D on the answer sheet.

Look at the following example:

X   Feature 16; update file list

This is an 'X' line, so look at the 'Rules for Building "X" lines'. Rule A has been broken, as there is no semi-colon at the end of the line. Rule B has been broken because the number 16 does not appear in brackets/parentheses. Therefore, circles A and B should be filled in, as below.

Example ● ● © Ⓓ

Time guideline: See how many of the following questions you can answer in 3 minutes.

Rules for Building 'X' lines	Rules for Building 'Y' lines
A Lines must end in a semi-colon	A Lines must begin with the word Comment
B Numbers must be in brackets/parantheses	B Numbers must be in quotation marks (i.e. ' ')
C All characters may be used except for # ' '	C All characters may be used except for . @ &

Remember, fill in circle D if no rules are broken.

Test 54 © SHL Group Plc 2005 SHL and OPQ are registered trademarks of SHL Group plc which are registered in the United Kingdom and other countries.

1   X   Set Var PQ to 10;

2   X   Change character set to 'modern' Greek;

3   Y   Comment Flag next 5 lines.

4   Y   Comment. Move (file) To Directory (new)

5   Y   Comment Read Value From Register (2);

6   X   Stop run if ABC < (23);

7   Y   Copy All Strings equal to '6' & '7' letters to buffer '1'

8   Y   Comment Let String – '10'

9   X   Allocate Demarcation (#) Bounds

10 Y   If A Greater Than 10, Replace Value A With Upper Value B

11 X   Enable's Automatic Printing, Speed # 200;

12 X   Cut file (XY) from line (8) to line 921;

Test 54 Answer Sheet

	A	B	C	D		A	B	C	D
1	Ⓐ	Ⓑ	Ⓒ	Ⓓ	7	Ⓐ	Ⓑ	Ⓒ	Ⓓ
2	Ⓐ	Ⓑ	Ⓒ	Ⓓ	8	Ⓐ	Ⓑ	Ⓒ	Ⓓ
3	Ⓐ	Ⓑ	Ⓒ	Ⓓ	9	Ⓐ	Ⓑ	Ⓒ	Ⓓ
4	Ⓐ	Ⓑ	Ⓒ	Ⓓ	10	Ⓐ	Ⓑ	Ⓒ	Ⓓ
5	Ⓐ	Ⓑ	Ⓒ	Ⓓ	11	Ⓐ	Ⓑ	Ⓒ	Ⓓ
6	Ⓐ	Ⓑ	Ⓒ	Ⓓ	12	Ⓐ	Ⓑ	Ⓒ	Ⓓ

Answers to Accuracy Tests questions

Test 44 Understanding Instructions

	A	B	C	D
1	●	B	C	D
2	A	●	C	D
3	A	B	●	D

Test 45 Basic Checking

	A	B	C	D	E
1	●	B	C	●	E
2	A	B	●	D	●
3	A	●	C	●	E
4	●	B	●	D	E
5	A	●	●	D	E
6	A	B	●	D	●
7	A	●	C	D	●
8	A	B	C	●	●
9	A	●	C	●	E
10	●	B	●	D	E
11	●	B	C	D	●
12	A	B	●	D	●
13	●	B	C	●	E
14	A	B	●	●	E

Test 46 Clerical Checking

	A	B	C	D	E
1	A	B	●	D	E
2	A	●	C	●	E
3	●	B	C	D	E
4	A	B	C	D	●
5	A	B	●	●	E
6	A	B	C	●	E
7	●	●	●	●	E
8	A	●	C	D	E
9	A	B	C	D	●
10	A	B	C	●	E
11	A	●	C	D	E
12	A	B	C	D	●
13	A	●	C	D	E
14	A	B	C	●	E
15	●	●	●	D	E

Test 47 Checking Information

	A	B	C	D	E
1	A	B	●	D	E
2	●	B	C	D	E
3	A	B	C	●	E

Test 48 Visual Checking

	A	B	C	D
1	A	●	C	D
2	●	B	C	D
3	A	B	C	●

Test 49 Computer Checking

	A	B	C	D	E
1	A	B	●	D	E
2	●	B	●	D	E
3	A	B	C	D	●
4	A	●	●	●	E

Test 50 Classification

	A	B	C	D	E
1	A	●	C	D	E
2	●	B	●	D	E
3	●	B	C	●	E
4	A	B	C	D	●
5	●	B	C	●	E
6	●	B	C	D	E
7	A	●	C	D	E
8	●	B	●	D	E
9	●	B	●	D	E
10	●	●	C	D	E
11	A	B	C	●	E
12	●	B	C	D	E

Test 51 Following Instructions

	A	B	C	D
1	A	●	C	D
2	A	B	●	D

Test 52 Coded Instructions

	A	B	C	D	E
1	Ⓐ	Ⓑ	●	Ⓓ	Ⓔ
2	Ⓐ	Ⓑ	Ⓒ	●	Ⓔ
3	Ⓐ	Ⓑ	Ⓒ	Ⓓ	●
4	Ⓐ	●	Ⓒ	Ⓓ	Ⓔ

Test 53 Computer Checking

	A	B	C	D	E
1	●	Ⓑ	Ⓒ	●	Ⓔ
2	Ⓐ	●	Ⓒ	Ⓓ	●
3	●	Ⓑ	●	Ⓓ	Ⓔ
4	Ⓐ	Ⓑ	Ⓒ	●	●
5	●	●	Ⓒ	Ⓓ	Ⓔ
6	Ⓐ	●	Ⓒ	●	Ⓔ
7	Ⓐ	Ⓑ	●	Ⓓ	●
8	●	Ⓑ	Ⓒ	Ⓓ	●
9	Ⓐ	●	Ⓒ	●	Ⓔ
10	Ⓐ	Ⓑ	●	●	Ⓔ
11	Ⓐ	●	Ⓒ	●	Ⓔ
12	Ⓐ	Ⓑ	●	●	Ⓔ
13	●	Ⓑ	Ⓒ	Ⓓ	●
14	Ⓐ	●	Ⓒ	Ⓓ	●
15	Ⓐ	Ⓑ	●	●	Ⓔ
16	●	Ⓑ	Ⓒ	●	Ⓔ
17	●	Ⓑ	Ⓒ	Ⓓ	●
18	Ⓐ	●	Ⓒ	Ⓓ	●
19	Ⓐ	●	Ⓒ	Ⓓ	●
20	Ⓐ	Ⓑ	Ⓒ	●	●

Test 54 Syntax Checking

	A	B	C	D
1	Ⓐ	●	Ⓒ	Ⓓ
2	Ⓐ	Ⓑ	●	Ⓓ
3	Ⓐ	●	●	Ⓓ
4	Ⓐ	Ⓑ	●	Ⓓ
5	Ⓐ	●	Ⓒ	Ⓓ
6	Ⓐ	Ⓑ	Ⓒ	●
7	●	Ⓑ	●	Ⓓ
8	Ⓐ	Ⓑ	Ⓒ	●
9	●	Ⓑ	●	Ⓓ
10	●	●	Ⓒ	Ⓓ
11	Ⓐ	●	●	Ⓓ
12	Ⓐ	●	Ⓒ	Ⓓ

Accuracy tests – how to improve your performance

- Use catalogues and timetables.

- Check the football or financial results.

- Play games involving checking numbers and letters.

- Read lots of instructions for using things, for example, digital clock, video recorder, washing machine, digital camera.

- Read lots of instructions for making or repairing things, for example, a cake, fixing a fuse, and check that you understand what you're reading.

- Try looking at manuals and instructions for games, appliances and computers.

- When you're studying the test material, try not to skip-read, or get distracted half way through.

Accuracy tests demand a very high level of concentration, so treat yourself to a short break every now and then. Sit up straight, shut your eyes and take a few deep breaths, just for 20 seconds or so. This will help you stay alert, relax you a little, and give your eyes and brain, a well deserved rest.

CHAPTER TEN

Combination Tests

So far, all the psychometric tests in this book have been very specific; each one of them measuring a certain ability, be it verbal, numerical, mechanical and so on.

However, out there in the big wide world, there are employers who do not use accredited and well researched psychometric tests from well established test publishers like SHL – they make up their own tests themselves. I have decided to include one of these tests.

It's what I call a *combination* test because it is a mixture of verbal reasoning, number problems and abstract puzzles, with one or two spatial reasoning questions thrown in for good measure. The company that uses it recruits graduates of the highest calibre into software engineering jobs.

Now, you might be thinking, 'How can a test like this sort out good software engineers from bad ones? How are these questions relevant to the IT industry?'

The answer is surprising – there isn't really any relevance at all! The company who uses this test isn't trying to measure verbal ability, nor numerical ability, nor general knowledge. What they are interested in is **speed of thought**. They want people who can think quickly.

In actual fact, speed of thought is an essential attribute for a software engineer. In a commercial world, projects completed quickly mean larger profits and an enhanced reputation for the company in question.

And there's another reason I've included this test – it's quite good fun!

Test 55 Combination Test

Instructions: The objective of the test is to answer correctly as many questions as possible in 12 minutes. Simply tick the letter corresponding to your answer underneath each question.

Although many of the questions are not particularly difficult, you'll need all the concentration you can muster to beat the clock, so sit somewhere quiet where you won't be disturbed.

Time guide: There are 44 questions. See how many you can do in 12 minutes. The answers are at the end of the chapter.

1   The 47th week of the year is in:

  (a) December
  (b) November
  (c) September
  (d) June
  (e) January

2   Does IQ stand for Intellectual Quotient?

  (a) Yes
  (b) No

3   Which word is different from the rest?

  (a) whimsical
  (b) playful
  (c) capricious
  (d) uncanny
  (e) comical

4   Pick the number that follows the pattern set by the series:

  0   1   3   6   10 __

  (a) 6
  (b) 14
  (c) 15
  (d) 16

5   Which one of these forms does not belong with the rest?

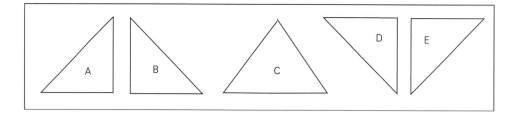

6   STRANGE is the opposite of:

(a)   similar
(b)   familiar
(c)   peculiar
(d)   obstinate
(e)   happy

7   One orange costs 12 pence. A dozen and a half oranges will cost:

(a)   £1.44
(b)   £2.16
(c)   £0.30
(d)   £1.80
(e)   £2.06

8   HARSH is the opposite of:

(a)   stern
(b)   mild
(c)   severe
(d)   warm
(e)   weather

9   OBVIOUS is the opposite of:

(a)   apparent
(b)   clear
(c)   obscure
(d)   visible
(e)   conspicuous

10   Which of the following numbers does not fit in with the pattern of this series?

64   54   42   31   20

(a)   64
(b)   54
(c)   42
(d)   31
(e)   20

11   Which one of these forms does not belong with the rest?

12   If most Gannucks are Dorks and most Gannucks are Xorgs, the statement that some Dorks are Xorgs is:

    (a)   True
    (b)   False
    (c)   Indeterminable from data

13   A car dealer spent £20,000 for some used cars. He sold them for £27,500 making an average of £1,500 on each car. How many cars did he sell?

    (a)   4
    (b)   11
    (e)   5
    (d)   15
    (e)   7

14   What is the opposite of ABDICATE?

    (a)   occupy
    (b)   edit
    (c)   court
    (d)   attempt
    (e)   abandon

15   If you put the following words into a meaningful statement, what would the last word be?

    (a)   fall
    (b)   a
    (c)   before
    (d)   pride
    (e)   comes

16   Which of the following words is related to SOUND as FOOD is to MOUTH?

    (a)   ear
    (b)   stomach
    (c)   music
    (d)   orchestra
    (e)   throat

17   Tom and Harry caught a dozen fish. Harry caught twice as many as Tom. How many did Tom catch?

    (a)   2
    (b)   4
    (c)   8
    (d)   6
    (e)   3

18 Which of the following numbers doesn't fit the sequence?

13 18 14 19 15 21 16

(a) 13
(b) 18
(c) 14
(d) 19
(e) 15
(f) 21
(g) 16

19 Which letter does not belong in the sequence?

C F J M Q U

(a) C
(b) F
(c) J
(d) M
(e) Q
(f) U

20 If George met Gertrude and Gertrude met Ralph, then the statement that George and Ralph did not meet is:

(a) True
(b) False
(c) Indeterminable

21 If it takes four bricklayers an hour to build a wall, how long will it take five of them to build the same wall?

(a) 90 minutes
(b) 45 minutes
(c) 50 minutes
(d) 48 minutes
(e) 40 minutes

22 What is the opposite of REPUDIATE?

(a) encourage
(b) crime
(c) endorse
(d) disappoint
(e) halt

23   The first four forms are alike in a certain way. Pick the numbered form that is also alike:

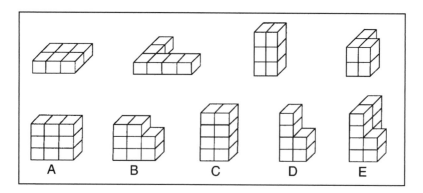

A   B   C   D   E

24   If Bob is older than Harry and Harry is older than Sue, the statement that Sue is younger than Bob is:

(a)   True
(b)   False
(c)   Indeterminable from data

25   What is the opposite of IMBUE?

(a)   prize
(b)   tasteful
(c)   texture
(d)   invest
(e)   clear

26   A bag of coffee beans costs £30 and contains 100 possible servings. However, typical wastage averages 25%. For how much must the proprietor sell a cup of coffee to make a 150% profit per bag?

(a)   £1.25
(b)   £0.75
(c)   £1.00
(d)   £2.00
(e)   none of these answers is right

27   If a pair of trousers takes one-and-a-half times as much cloth as a shirt, and the total cloth used for the trousers and the shirt costs £50, how much does the cloth for the trousers cost?

(a)   £25
(b)   £20
(c)   £30
(d)   £40
(e)   none of these answers

28   Complete the comparison: BOOK is to LIBRARY as PAINTING is to

   (a)   artists
   (b)   curator
   (c)   easel
   (d)   gallery
   (e)   building

29   What meaning do the following two statements have?

   Don't put all your eggs in one basket.
   Don't count your chickens before they hatch.

   (a)   same
   (b)   opposite
   (c)   neither the same nor opposite

30   Which one of the following numbers doesn't fit the pattern?

   5/8   9/24   1/4   2/16   0

   (a)   5/8
   (b)   9/24
   (c)   1/4
   (d)   2/16
   (e)   0

31   Complete the comparison: BISHOP is to CHESS as SOLDIER is to

   (a)   battlefield
   (b)   war
   (c)   government
   (d)   army
   (e)   gun

32   Pick the piece that's missing from the puzzle.

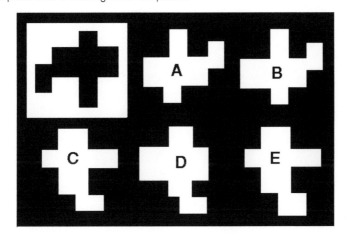

33 The following statements:

Hindsight is always 20/20
Can't see the trees for the forest

(a) are the same in meaning
(b) are opposite in meaning
(c) are neither the same nor opposite in meaning

34 A zoo has some lions and some ostriches. The zoo keeper counted 15 heads and 50 legs. How many lions were there?

(a) 9
(b) 10
(c) 11
(d) 12
(e) 13
(f) 14

35 A sushi restaurant buys twenty fish for £10 each. The owner knows that 50% of the fish will go bad before being served. Each fish creates 10 servings. What price must they charge per serving in order to make a 100% profit on their initial investment?

(a) £4
(b) £2
(c) £3
(d) £6
(e) £20

36 The words SURREPTITIOUS and SUSPICIOUS mean:

(a) same
(b) opposite
(c) neither the same nor opposite

37 Three partners venture on a project. They pro-rate their (potential) profits over their £11,000 investment. Dan invests twice as much as Pete. Pete invests 50% more than Phil. If the venture breaks even how much does Phil get back?

(a) £6000
(b) £2500
(c) £2000
(d) £3666.66
(e) 0

38   A basketball player shoots 33% from the foul line. How many shots must he take to make 100 baskets?

   (a)   300
   (b)   301
   (c)   304
   (d)   100
   (e)   333

39   All Nerds are Jerks and some Nerds are Geeks. A few Geeks are BrainMasters, therefore all Brainmasters are Jerks.

   (a)   True
   (b)   False
   (c)   Indeterminable from data

40   A submarine averages 10 miles an hour under water and 25 miles per hour on the surface. How many hours will it take it to make a 350 mile trip if it goes two-and-a-half times further on the surface?

   (a)   10
   (b)   15
   (c)   35
   (d)   20
   (e)   65

41   A man was given eight pound coins. However, one of them was fake and he did not know if the fake coin weighed more or less than the other coins. What is the minimum number of weighings that it would take to guarantee him finding the counterfeit coin? Assume a balance scale is used.

   (a)   2
   (b)   3
   (c)   7
   (d)   12
   (e)   Indeterminable from data

42   Which number does not fit within the following sequence?

   1/5 1/6   1/8   1/10 1/15   1/30

   (a)   1/5
   (b)   1/6
   (c)   1/8
   (d)   1/10
   (e)   1/15
   (f)   1/30

43 At the end of a banquet 10 people shake hands with each other. How many handshakes will there be in total?

    (a) 100
    (b) 90
    (c) 45
    (d) 20
    (e) 50

44 Complete the comparison: SOLICITOR is to ADVISER as SYCOPHANT is to:

    (a) ruffian
    (b) fawner
    (c) nobleman
    (d) blackmailer
    (e) flautist

Answers to combination test

Now here are the answers. For your information, the company who uses this test considers a score of 30 or more *correct* answers good enough to move a candidate on to the next stage in the recruitment process. No one has ever scored full marks.

1 b	23 d
2 b	24 a
3 d	25 e
4 c	26 c
5 c	27 c
6 b	28 d
7 b	29 c
8 b	30 a
9 c	31 b
10 b	32 c
11 c	33 c
12 a	34 b
13 c	35 a
14 a	36 c
15 a	37 c
16 a	38 c
17 b	39 c
18 f	40 d
19 f	41 b
20 c	42 c
21 d	43 c
22 c	44 b

CHAPTER ELEVEN

Personality Questionnaires

What are personality questionnaires?

Personality questionnaires are psychometric tests which assess the different aspects of personality and character relevant to the world of work, for example:

✓ motivation
✓ thinking style
✓ problem solving
✓ preferred working style
✓ feelings and emotions
✓ business awareness
✓ interpersonal skills
✓ leadership ability
✓ managerial, professional or entrepreneurial qualities
✓ communication skills.

However, personality questionnaires, or 'inventories' or 'self report forms' as they are sometimes called, are not tests in the true sense of the word, for two reasons:

1. there are no right or wrong answers
2. they are not timed.

What they are, though, is popular. Written by occupational psychologists and administered by trained HR personnel, their use has increased dramatically in the last few years. From shelf-stacker to managing director, apply for a job with any medium to large organisation (commercial or otherwise) and I can virtually guarantee you will be asked to complete one or more personality questionnaire.

The results of the personality questionnaire could determine your overall suitability to work for a particular organisation, or place you in an appropriate department, or team, once the decision has already been made to employ you. They're also very useful for recruiters, because it gives them something to talk about when they interview you.

Used in conjunction with ability-type tests, personality questionnaires can give an employer a pretty accurate assessment of how well you would be suited to a particular job.

There are **two** main types of personality questionnaire. The first is often referred to in HR jargon as a 'competency' questionnaire.

Competency questionnaires

Competency questionnaires tend to be pretty short, and they focus on behavioural actions, which are things like:

◆ Managerial qualities (leadership, planning, organisation, attention to detail and persuasiveness).

◆ Professional qualities (specialist knowledge, problem solving, analytical ability, oral and written communication).

◆ Entrepreneurial qualities (commercial awareness, creativity, understanding of the need to plan for the longer term).

◆ Personal qualities (an ability to work well with other people, flexibility, resilience and motivation).

Competency questionnaires are frequently used on application forms and online application forms. Here's an example of the sort of question you might get:

I am the sort of person who...

1   A   Easily establishes rapport with reports.

         B   Influences the course of meetings.

         C   Speaks coherently.

         D   Encourages colleagues to meet objectives.

2   A   Writes creatively.

         B   Seeks answers to problems.

         C   Is effective in communicating requirements.

         D   Is aware of costs.

For each question you have to decide which statement is the most like you and also which is the least like you – not an easy task.

Competency-type questions are also a favourite with interviewers who, analysing the answers you gave on the application form test, like to hit you with questions like:

'*Tell me about a situation in which you influenced the course of a meeting.*'

You can see what they're getting at – they want to know how you behave in the work situation.

The way competency questionnaires are scored is that generally, each organisation using them chooses a small number of qualities which they feel are essential to the particular job, and use these to put together their own unique scoring key. Very sensible actually, since nobody in the world has all the qualities listed above.

So if you are rejected by a company on the basis of an application form test, don't worry. You might be the 'wrong' sort of person for them, but perfect for the next company you apply to. I'd say it's best to forget about the scoring mechanism and just answer as honestly as you can, because it's in your interest to do so.

True personality questionnaires

True personality questionnaires are usually much longer than competency-type questionnaires. For example, one version of SHL's very well known OPQ32, which asks you to answer questions in a similar format to the Making Choices test shown below, has 108 pages!

Personality questionnaires are generally used when you go along to be interviewed, when you attend an assessment centre, and they are often completed online. The SHL tests are scored by measuring the test result against 32 different dimensions of personality. These include:

◆ Relationships with people (how persuasive, controlling, outgoing, modest, caring, democratic, independently minded, confident or outspoken you are).

◆ Your thinking style (how rational, evaluative, conventional, conceptual, innovative, forward thinking, detail conscious, conscientious or rule following you are).

◆ Your feelings and emotions (how relaxed, worrying, tough minded, optimistic, trusting, emotionally controlled, vigorous, competitive, achieving or decisive you are).

All of these 'dimensions' are related to how you behave in the workplace.

How can personality questionnaires be valid when you rate yourself?

Recruiting organisations are fully aware that personality questionnaires reveal only your *perception* of yourself, which isn't necessarily the same thing as the way other people see you. However, the tests are very sophisticated, and in most cases (as I have found out recently myself) frighteningly accurate.

Will I be asked any very personal questions?

No. Personality questionnaires are not puzzles or quizzes of the magazine variety; they never ask you about your favourite foods or your love life. The personality questionnaires used in recruitment simply assess aspects of your personality and character as they relate to the working environment, or a specific job.

What sort of questions will I be asked?

To give you a flavour of what to expect I have included two different practice personality questionnaires for you to try. As mentioned above, the only difference between these tests and the real thing is that real-life personality questionnaires have a lot more questions. Try to answer the questions honestly and accurately – it's not easy, as you will see.

Test 56 Rating Statements

In this test you are asked to rate yourself on a number of different phrases or statements. After reading each statement mark your answer according to the following rules:

Fill in circle 1 — If you strongly disagree with the statement
Fill in circle 2 — If you disagree with the statement
Fill in circle 3 — If you are unsure
Fill in circle 4 — If you agree with the statement
Fill in circle 5 — If you strongly agree with the statement

The first statement has already been completed for you. The person has agreed that 'I enjoy meeting new people' is an accurate description of him/herself.
  Now try questions 2 to 6 for yourself by completely filling in the circle that is most true for you.

		Strongly disagree	Disagree	Unsure	Agree	Strongly agree
1	I enjoy meeting new people	①	②	③	●	⑤
2	I like helping people	①	②	③	④	⑤
3	I sometimes make mistakes	①	②	③	④	⑤
4	I don't mind taking risks	①	②	③	④	⑤
5	I'm easily disappointed	①	②	③	④	⑤
6	I enjoy repairing things	①	②	③	④	⑤

Test 57 Making Choices

This personality questionnaire is similar to the well known SHL OPQ32. For each question you are given a block of four statements: A, B, C and D. You must choose the statement which you think is *most* true or typical of you in your everyday behaviour, and you must **also** choose the statement which is *least* true or typical of you.

Indicate your choices by filling in the appropriate circle in the row marked 'M' (for most) and in the next row 'L' (for least).

The first question has been completed as an example of what to do. The person has chosen, '*I feel relaxed*' as most true or typical, and '*I am organised*' as being least true or typical. Now try the rest yourself, thinking carefully before you answer.

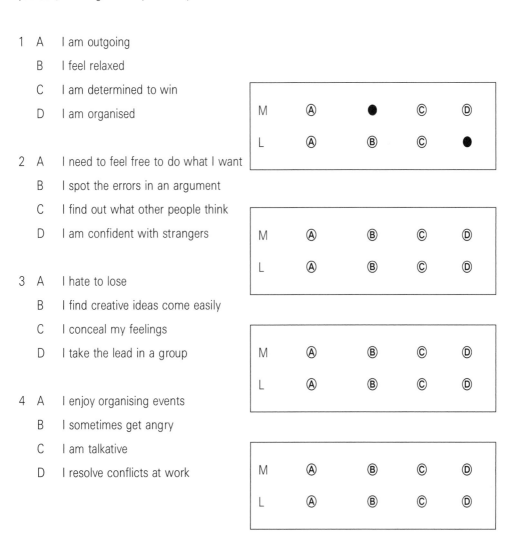

1   A   I am outgoing

   B   I feel relaxed

   C   I am determined to win

   D   I am organised

2   A   I need to feel free to do what I want

   B   I spot the errors in an argument

   C   I find out what other people think

   D   I am confident with strangers

3   A   I hate to lose

   B   I find creative ideas come easily

   C   I conceal my feelings

   D   I take the lead in a group

4   A   I enjoy organising events

   B   I sometimes get angry

   C   I am talkative

   D   I resolve conflicts at work

5 A   I am seldom quiet

    B   I focus on underlying concepts

    C   I am free of tension

    D   I sell a new idea well

M	Ⓐ	Ⓑ	Ⓒ	Ⓓ
L	Ⓐ	Ⓑ	Ⓒ	Ⓓ

6 A   I enjoy variety

    B   I am highly active

    C   I get the details right

    D   I am effective in negotiations

M	Ⓐ	Ⓑ	Ⓒ	Ⓓ
L	Ⓐ	Ⓑ	Ⓒ	Ⓓ

7 A   I help people with their problems

    B   I develop new approaches

    C   I have lots of energy

    D   I enjoy social activities

M	Ⓐ	Ⓑ	Ⓒ	Ⓓ
L	Ⓐ	Ⓑ	Ⓒ	Ⓓ

8 A   I keep paperwork in order

    B   I need to win

    C   I insist on doing this my own way

    D   I get worried before a big meeting

M	Ⓐ	Ⓑ	Ⓒ	Ⓓ
L	Ⓐ	Ⓑ	Ⓒ	Ⓓ

9 A   I have a wide circle of friends

    B   I enjoy organising people

    C   I relax easily

    D   I seek variety

M	Ⓐ	Ⓑ	Ⓒ	Ⓓ
L	Ⓐ	Ⓑ	Ⓒ	Ⓓ

10 A   I am lively in conversation

B   I follow rules and regulations

C   I persevere with tasks

D   I avoid talking about my successes

	M	Ⓐ	Ⓑ	Ⓒ	
Ⓓ					
L	Ⓐ	Ⓑ	Ⓒ	Ⓓ	

11 A   I like statistical analysis

B   I take a conventional approach

C   I draw immediate conclusions

D   I rarely lose or misplace things

	M	Ⓐ	Ⓑ	Ⓒ	Ⓓ
	L	Ⓐ	Ⓑ	Ⓒ	Ⓓ

12 A   I think consultation is essential

B   I am tense before an important meeting

C   I vary my behaviour according to the situation

D   I enjoy taking the lead

	M	Ⓐ	Ⓑ	Ⓒ	Ⓓ
	L	Ⓐ	Ⓑ	Ⓒ	Ⓓ

13 A   I enjoy bargaining with someone

B   I take time to be supportive

C   I speak up when people are wrong

D   I quickly draw conclusions

	M	Ⓐ	Ⓑ	Ⓒ	Ⓓ
	L	Ⓐ	Ⓑ	Ⓒ	Ⓓ

14 A   I enjoy talking to new people

B   I rarely keep things tidy

C   I like to help others

D   I worry about deadlines

	M	Ⓐ	Ⓑ	Ⓒ	Ⓓ
	L	Ⓐ	Ⓑ	Ⓒ	Ⓓ

What if I can't decide which statement is *least* like me?

I agree, it is difficult. In the past, when you took a personality test, there would always be several answer choices which stood out a mile as being the wrong ones. But not any more.

Here are some other examples of statements taken from personality questionnaires:

◆ Changes tasks willingly and grasps new ideas quickly.
◆ Communicates equally well with customers and colleagues.
◆ Pursues tasks energetically.
◆ Shares all relevant and useful information with the team.

You can see the problem. Which of these statements should you choose as being the *least* like you? They all describe qualities you'd imagine any employer would find highly desirable.

This test, and others like it are extremely clever because they are impossible to fudge. There are no obvious right or wrong answers. And the fact that there are no blindingly obvious 'least like you' answers, forces you to think hard about yourself and be honest.

And that's exactly what organisations who use these tests want – honesty.

Note: you may also have problems deciding which statements are *most* like you!

Is it possible to cheat?

Modern personality questionnaires have sophisticated built-in mechanisms which can spot any deliberate lying or inconsistency easily. If you try to second-guess the examiners by picking the answers you think they're looking for, your questionnaire is likely to be regarded as invalid, and your application rejected. Your only choice is to answer the questions as truthfully and honestly as you can.

The tests also have a huge number of questions and the sheer size of the questionnaire makes it even more difficult to lie consistently – it might be possible at the beginning, but by the 100th question it'll be difficult to remember your own name, let alone which qualities you're pretending to possess.

Besides, personality questionnaires are also about fitting the right people into the right jobs. By answering honestly, you're more likely to land a job that you enjoy and can do well.

Are there any other types of personality questionnaire?

In this chapter I have covered competency and personality questionnaires, however you could also be asked to complete an **interest inventory**, which is a questionnaire in which you are asked to decide how much you like various types of activities at work.

You could also come across something called a **motivation questionnaire** which looks at the energy with which you approach your work, and the different conditions which increase or decrease your motivation. Personally I think that as far as motivation is concerned, your employer has a lot to answer for!

Personality questionnaires – how to improve your performance

With every other type of psychometric test I have been able to give you some suggestions as to how to improve your performance; however with personality questionnaires, there are no tricks of the trade or useful exercises to practise. As I have already said, the most important thing to do is to *be yourself*. Remember:

◆ Personality and competency questionnaires do not have right or wrong answers. You don't have to worry about passing or failing – just concentrate on being honest, truthful and accurate.

◆ Make sure you answer all the questions. There may seem a lot of them, but it *is* necessary to complete the whole test.

◆ Personality questionnaires do not have time limits, but try to work your way through reasonably quickly. This is particularly useful when being asked to decide which 'qualities' are most or least like you, as intuitive answers are usually the most accurate.

- Some questions may seem irrelevant. Don't worry about this. Just answer as truthfully as you can and move on. The same goes for questions you don't fully understand. Do your best and don't leave any of the answers blank.

- Many questions ask you about the way you behave in a work situation. If you have no formal work experience, think about how you behave in similar situation at university or college or in other areas of your life.

- As mentioned above, many big firms actually list the personality traits they look for in their employees on their websites. Treat this information as a useful guide but don't try to second-guess the examiner – always be honest.

- After you've finished the test, you might have second thoughts about some of your responses. For example, after taking the *OPQ32* I suddenly realised that rating all the 'I plan ahead' type statements as *least* like me was totally inaccurate; I should have chosen *most* like me instead! Everyone does this, but be assured it doesn't seem to affect the test results greatly.

After taking a personality questionnaire, you should be offered the chance to discuss the results (and if the offer is not forthcoming, ask). Use the opportunity to find out as much about yourself as you can. Even if you are not offered that particular job, a better understanding of your strengths and limitations is always useful.

PART THREE
What Else Do Psychometrics Tests Measure?

CHAPTER TWELVE

What Else Do Psychometric Tests Measure?

As you have seen, there are many different types of psychometric test. Some measure your ability to work or reason in a certain way, some claim to analyse aspects of your personality and character.

But there are three things that **all** psychometric tests measure.

- Firstly, your ability to concentrate and work hard for a reasonable amount of time.

- Secondly, your ability (or lack of it) to follow instructions and work neatly – absolutely essential if you want to score any points at all on any kind of psychometric test.

- And lastly, of course, your ability to understand precisely what you are being asked to do.

These are qualities **every** organisation looks for in its staff. They want your timekeeping to be reliable. They want you to be able to settle down and work quickly and effectively and not mess about. They want you to respect the organisation's culture and follow laid-down procedures, not make up your own rules as you go along. They want you to get on with your job and not waste time pretending to be ill, gossiping or playing computer games.

Asking a bit much, I suppose, but some people are unable (or unwilling) to do any of these things.

Your references may not be entirely honest. Your CV may exaggerate your achievements. But with a psychometric test, you are on your own. You can see why employers like them so much.

And lastly...

I hope you have enjoyed working your way through this practice book. Psychometric tests are now an extremely important part of the recruitment process, but the good news is that once you've got through the initial stages of a selection process (which shouldn't be a problem now) you will always have your chance to impress at an interview. And at an interview, that's where you can let your enthusiasm for the job and the company itself, shine through.

Speaking of enthusiasm, that's the one thing that psychometric tests cannot measure. Personally, I think that getting in on time every day and giving your all are to a large extent determined by how much you enjoy the actual work, how well you get on with your colleagues, and how decent your boss is. Perhaps they should invent psychometric tests for employers – now that's a book I'd like to write!

CHAPTER THIRTEEN

Resources

Help and information on the Internet

www.psychometrics.co.uk

Interesting information about psychometric tests, assessment centres, CV writing etc.

www.shldirect.com

Easy-to-navigate site includes careers guidance, help with the assessment process and free practice ability tests and personality questionnaires.

www.brain.com

Lots of free IQ, acuity and memory tests plus lots of articles on brain topics.

www.ase-solutions.co.uk

Example abstract, verbal and numerical questions, plus practice questions for their best known psychometric tests – GMA, 16PF5, FGA (First Graduate Assessment), GAT2 and MOST.

www.advisorteam.com

Take the free Keirsey Temperament Sorter and discover whether you are an Artisan, Guardian, Rational or Idealist. Also IQ tests and a free newsletter.

www.testingroom.com

US site offering free tests on topics such as personality, career values, career interest inventories and career competencies.

www.majon.com/iq.html

Another interesting US site includes an IQ test selection area, with information on the main US postgraduate college entrance exams (all high-level psychometric tests) including GRE, LSAT, GMAT, MCAT and SAT.

www.morrisby.com

Includes nine pages of sample questions covering: Abstract, Verbal, Numerical, Perceptual, Shape and Mechanical tests.

www.9types.com

Entertaining personality questionnaire site.

http://www.outofservice.com/

All sorts of personality tests, not particularly work-based but good fun nevertheless.

www.prospects.ac.uk

Extensive site for graduates, with loads of career and job-hunting advice, plus jobs.

www.careersa-z.co.uk

Information on hundreds of different careers.

http://work.guardian.co.uk

Great interactive job site has free practice psychometric tests plus lots of work-related news.

www.jobserve.com

Good recruitment site for a multitude of different industries, especially IT.

www.hotrecruit.co.uk

Thousands of part-time and temporary jobs, including lots of extraordinary and simply crazy jobs.

Further reading

Be Prepared!, Julie-Ann Amos (How To Books, 2004). How to develop the confidence to succeed – research the company, understand the golden rules of body language and control your nerves.

CVs for High Flyers, Rachel Bishop-Firth (How To Books, 2004). How to make the most of your experience and turn perceived weak points to your advantage.

Graduate Career Directory (Hobsons, published yearly). Career and job hunting advice, plus hundreds of employer profiles.

Handling Tough Job Interviews, Julie-Ann Amos (How To Books, 2004). Preparation for interviews with; recruitment agencies, headhunters, employers or human resources departments.

High Powered CVs, Rachel Bishop-Firth (How To Books, 2004). Powerful application strategies to get you that senior level job.

Landing Your First Job, Andrea Shavick (Kogan Page).

Passing Psychometric Tests, Andrea Shavick (How To Books, 2002). How to pass the tests, whether you're a school leaver, a graduate, already working or a returner.

Psychometric Tests for Graduates, Andrea Shavick (How To Books, 2003). Graduate-level psychometric and management tests.

Succeeding at Interviews, Judith Verity (How To Books, 2004). Give great answers and ask the right questions.

Successful Interviews Every Time, Dr Rob Yeung (How To Books, 2004). Never be caught out by any interview question ever again.

Turn Your Degree into a Career, Dr Michael Collins and Benjamin Scott (How To Books, 2003). Job finding techniques that have actually been proven to work for undergraduates and postgraduates.

The Job Application Handbook, Judith Johnstone (How To Books, 2004). The best ways to approach potential employers.

Write a Great CV, Paul McGee (How To Books, 2001). Interview preparation tips, sample job ads, action plans, specimen CVs and covering letters.

Index

If you want to know how ... to handle tough job interviews

'Job interviews can be daunting, because often there is our livelihood at stake. A little preparation and understanding about how interviews work can help. Even better is understanding the purpose of the different stages of interview in a recruitment process, and the balance of power in those interviews.

'This book is about understanding why you are there, and what to do when things get difficult. It's about knowing your way through the recruitment process so that each hurdle is cleared to get you the job you want – if it's right for you.'

Julie-Ann Amos

Handling Tough Job Interviews
Be prepared, perform well, get the job
Julie-Ann Amos

'A wealth of sound advice.' – Sesame (Open University magazine)

'Takes you step-by-step through the recruitment process and gives useful advice on interviews with senior management, dealing with psychometric tests; and discussing and agreeing the job offer.' – Office Secretary

'Its strength is that it covers all kinds of interview from recruitment agencies and headhunters to employer and human resources.' – Phoenix Magazine

ISBN 1 85703 845 2

If you want to know how ... to pass psychometric tests

Over 95% of FTSE 100 companies use psychometric testing to select their staff; as do the police, the Civil Service, local authorities, the Armed Forces, the Fire Service, financial institutions, retail companies, the communications industry, the motor industry, the power industry – the list is endless. In fact, the vast majority of large-medium sized organisations use psychometric tests to recruit. So if you're looking for a job you need to know what to expect. This book gives you the information, confidence and practice to do that, and more.

Passing Psychometric Tests
Know what to expect and get the job you want
Andrea Shavick

'An insightful book.' – The Guardian

'A very good aid for those who might find themselves facing a psychometric questionnaire.' – Irish Examiner

ISBN 1 85703 819 3

If you want to know how ... to excel at graduate level psychometric tests

'Unfortunately the days when all you needed was a great CV and a sparkling performance at interview are long gone. Now you also need to be able to pass a whole range of psychometric and management tests with flying oclours. That's what this book is all about. It explains all there is to know about the tests; what they are, what they measure, who uses them, why they're used, how to survive them, and of coure, how to pass them with flying colours!'

Andrea Shavick

Psychometric Tests for Graduates

Gain the confidence you need to excel at graduate-level psychometric and management tests

Andrea Shavick

This book contains 37 genuine graduate-level practice tests from SHL Group plc, the biggest test publisher in the world; 227 questions covering verbal, numerical, abstract and spatial reasoning, mechanical comprehension, fault diagnosis, accuracy and personality; and genuine practice *Brainstorm*, *Scenarios* and *Fastrack* management tests. Research methods are also covered.

ISBN 1 85703 911 4

If you want to know how ... to prepare for interviews

'It's the interviewer's prerogative to throw just about any question they can think of at the interviewee. So you might think that it's almost impossible to prepare for an interview. But the truth is that 80% of interview questions revolve around 20 common themes. And many interviewees let themselves down by not thinking about these themes, preparing and rehearsing responses to them.

'Many candidates then go on to create a wrong impression. Remember that an interviewer has to *like* you and warm to you as a person, as well as want to work with you because you answer the questions well. I see too many candidates who talk too much or come across as nervous or unfriendly. If you get the chance to rehearse with a friend and get some feedback on just how you come across, you will improve your chances no end.'

Rob Yeung

Successful Interviews Every Time
Rob Yeung

'*Successful Interviews* is the type of book that one may not wish to share with others who are job seeking in competition with oneself. Nevertheless, I owe a debt of gratitude to Dr Rob Yeung for sharing his experiences with us...' – *S. Lewis, Coventry*

'This book is an invaluable source of information for job hunters on preparing for interviews, tests and assessment centres.' – *Jonathan Turpin, Chief Executive of job hunting website fish4jobs.co.uk*

ISBN 1 85703 978 5